BE A
DIRECT SELLING
SUPERSTAR

BE A
DIRECT SELLING
SUPERSTAR

Achieve Financial Freedom for Yourself
and Others as a Direct Sales Leader

Mary Christensen

᠍AMACOM

American Management Association

New York • Atlanta • Brussels • Chicago • Mexico City
San Francisco • Shanghai • Tokyo • Toronto • Washington, D.C.

This publication is designed to provide accurate and authoritative information in regard to the subject matter covered. It is sold with the understanding that the publisher is not engaged in rendering legal, accounting, or other professional service. If legal advice or other expert assistance is required, the services of a competent professional person should be sought.

Library of Congress Cataloging-in-Publication Data

Christensen, Mary, 1951–
  Be a direct selling superstar : achieve financial freedom for yourself and others
      as a direct sales leader / Mary Christensen.
    pages cm
  Includes index.
  ISBN-13: 978-0-8144-3207-5 (pbk.)
  ISBN-10: 0-8144-3207-7 (pbk.)
  1. Direct selling. 2. Sales management. 3. Leadership. I. Title.
  HF5438.25.C51247 2013
  658.8'72—dc23
                              2012045570

About AMA
American Management Association (www.amanet.org) is a world leader in talent development, advancing the skills of individuals to drive business success. Our mission is to support the goals of individuals and organizations through a complete range of products and services, including classroom and virtual seminars, webcasts, webinars, podcasts, conferences, corporate and government solutions, business books, and research. AMA's approach to improving performance combines experiential learning—learning through doing—with opportunities for ongoing professional growth at every step of one's career journey.

Printing number

10 9 8 7 6 5 4 3 2 1

For Nikki and David.
I love you and I'm so proud of you.

Thanks to my publishers, AMACOM, especially my editor, Ellen Kadin, and Therese Mausser for driving my books into new markets around the world.

CONTENTS

★ PART TWO: TEAM LEADERSHIP

★ PART THREE: BUSINESS LEADERSHIP

BE A
DIRECT SELLING
SUPERSTAR

Introduction

The magic of a direct selling business is that it allows you to control your own income. And when you control your income you control your life. By building a direct selling business you can achieve a lifestyle most people only dream about. And you'll do so by helping others achieve the income and lifestyle they dream about.

Income on the sales your business generates will be just the start. Cash bonuses, exotic travel, luxury cars, expensive jewelry, and tax benefits are all part of the package. You'll form lifetime friendships with excited and exciting people.

By growing financially you'll expand your horizons. Direct selling is a personal growth business, and it is impossible to grow your business without growing yourself. Whatever product you represent, or corporation you partner with, this book will equip you to promote to the highest levels of your compensation plan.

Millions have traveled the path you're on, and reached the elite levels where the most exciting rewards await. You won't have to blaze your own trail, as they have already discovered everything you need to know. All you have to do is follow their footsteps.

Success comes from making the right moves at the right time, and now is the time to build your direct selling business. Here's why:

1. While owning a business has always been the American dream, crippling costs topple the majority of these businesses before they start making a profit. From interest on money borrowed to get the business started, to rent, utilities, inventory, and wages to keep it running, the bills keep coming whether the business is generating income or not. Losses through customers who default on their payments, as well as shrinkage through theft, damage, and obsolescence, make it harder to profit in good times, let alone tough times.

In direct selling, the lion's share of the investment comes from the corporation you partner with. You won't have to use your personal savings to fund your business, or incur significant costs to run it. By taking advantage of the significant tax breaks available to home-based entrepreneurs, you'll keep more of what you earn.

2. This century's economic wake-up calls have spun attitudes toward employment 180 degrees. Workers who used to seek security in employment now accept the fact that the only security is self-reliance. Direct selling is the ideal solution for anyone who wants to control his or her paycheck, not live with the frustration of subsidizing lazy coworkers or the fear of being laid off, forced to take a pay cut, or denied a raise.

Professions that reward seniority over performance are driving many talented workers to self-employment. The last-on-first-off policy that exists in teaching is a case in point. Many former teachers who are now successful leaders in direct selling cite job uncertainty as the key factor in switching careers, and they are happy to find that their training and skills can be utilized just as effectively in direct selling as they were in teaching.

In direct selling there's no discrimination based on longevity or on any other factor. You get to call the shots on when you work, where you work, and with whom you work. You won't have to work with people you don't like, or compete with coworkers for promotion. The better your performance is, the higher your paycheck will be.

3. Smart technologies equip you to run your businesses with resources that equal those of any large corporation. By taking care of the back end of the business, the corporation frees you to work the front line, where you'll generate your income. Tasks that used to consume time, from keeping in touch with customers, prospects, and team members to placing and delivering orders, tracking performance, and staying informed, are now performed at the click of a button. You can be at the ballpark with your kids or on the treadmill at your gym and still check on your business in an instant.

4. Because direct sellers are independent contractors, the profession attracts a wide range of ages, ambitions, and experiences. You'll find young entrepreneurs who are shunning traditional employment in search of freedom and flexibility as well as experienced workers who are tired of playing office politics. You'll find career professionals who have climbed the corporate ladder only to realize it's leaning against the wrong wall, and mom-preneurs who want to achieve a balance of earning an income while raising a family.

Census figures explain why direct selling is a magnet for women. With shocking inequalities, such as women earning seventy-seven cents for every dollar a man earns, it comes as little surprise that women account for more than 80 percent of all direct sellers.

Many ambitious women are waking up to the fact that discrimination gets worse the higher they climb. Ten years after graduating from college, women can expect to earn sixty-nine cents for the same job their male classmates are paid a dollar to do. CNNMoney.com reports that only twelve Fortune 500 companies are currently headed by women CEOs, and only 16 percent of Fortune 500 corporations have female board members. Direct selling does not favor one gender over another. The cream rises to the top.

5. A direct selling business is mobile. Whereas retail stores have the mobility of a stalled car, direct selling is a high-performance vehicle in motion. Direct sellers take their business direct to their customers, instead of waiting for customers to come to them. They do in-home presentations to showcase their products to shoppers who are bored with the monotony of malls. They buy each other's products and attract new prospects at trade shows and fairs. They create contacts in their community by speaking at clubs and professional associations, and sponsoring events and fund-raisers.

6. As a direct seller, you're in business *for* yourself but not *by* yourself. You'll receive all the support you need from your corporate partner and from the person who sponsored you into the business, and in turn you'll experience immense satisfaction from helping the people you sponsor. You'll spend your time with people who aspire to have more, do more, and be more in their lives, as you do. Their energy and excitement will kindle yours, and their successes will inspire you to reach higher.

With more than two thousand direct selling corporations to choose from, each with unique products and services, direct selling offers an opportunity for everyone. According to the Direct Selling Association (dsa.org), there are more than fifteen million direct sellers in America. Many countries, including Canada, Australia, and South Africa, have more than one million, and there are more than a hundred million worldwide. Explosive growth in China, Central America, South America, Europe, and many emerging economies has created a true global business opportunity that you can take advantage of from your own home.

7. Few workers can afford the luxury of an abrupt career change, but aspiring entrepreneurs can start a direct selling business while working their full-time job. The opportunity to build a business by working part-time or even in your spare time gives the profession an edge over most opportunities. "I'm working toward replacing my paycheck" is a goal shared by many aspiring direct selling entrepreneurs.

Twenty-five thousand people sign a direct selling agreement in America every single day, and one hundred thousand sign on worldwide. The number is escalating as a groundswell of desire for freedom, flexibility, and a family-first lifestyle fuels the demand for self-employment opportunities. And that spells opportunity for you. Every one of these people—small and large producers alike—will join an organization led by someone like you, and contribute to the sales that determine your income. The larger your network of sellers, and the more they sell, the more you'll earn. Even your smallest producers can add up to significant residual income over time.

There are many reasons why I love direct selling, but the most powerful is that your income and rewards will be directly related to how successful you are at helping others identify, pursue, and attain their goals. The rewards you enjoy will be greater than the income you earn. As you climb to the summit of your compensation plan you'll shine a light that inspires others to set their sights higher.

Every successful direct selling leader automatically becomes a role model for those who aspire to improve their lives.

Are you ready to reap the rewards that the highest-paid leaders enjoy?

To grow, lead, and manage a profitable, long-term direct selling business, you must master seven key skills in each of the three key areas of leadership, as explained in the three sections of this book:

1. Personal Leadership
2. Team Leadership
3. Business Leadership

Success does not come from a visit by the good-luck fairy. It comes from learning the skills and putting them to work.

You'll know whether you have the mindset of an elite leader by your answers to three simple questions:

Am I willing to work?
Am I willing to learn?
Am I willing to be paid for my results?

If you answered yes, yes, and yes, you're prequalified for success. Welcome to your journey toward becoming one of direct selling's highest paid achievers. It's time to get your journey started.

PART ONE

Personal
Leadership

*As you build your business you'll transform
many lives. Start by transforming your own.*
—MARY CHRISTENSEN

CHAPTER ONE

Find Your Passion

You cannot be inspiring unless you're inspired.
—MARY CHRISTENSEN

Direct selling is a personal growth business. Most of us are drawn to it because we want to improve our lives. Some of us dream of the financial freedom to do anything we want for the rest of our life, without counting the cost. Others dream of traveling the world, owning a ski lodge in the mountains, or sending our children to the best schools. The only limit to our dreams is our imagination.

Whether your dreams are financial, social, educational, or emotional, keep them alive with images on your screensaver or dream board. But focus your attention on the present.

The drawback to dreams is they have no time limit. When there's no deadline it's tempting to postpone taking action today. That's why we set goals.

Goals are the stepping-stones to our dreams. Each goal we achieve takes us one step closer to the lifestyle we dream about. However, each goal is also a destination in itself, one we can reach in a fairly short time. Whether it's paying a bill, buying a boat, taking a vacation, or eliminating debt, the maximum time frame for a goal should be twelve months.

Goals have an urgency that powers us forward, despite any doubts, disappointments, or distractions we encounter along the way. They stop us becoming discouraged or defeated when things don't go according to plan. They give us the strength to get back on our feet and back in the game after a knockdown.

As a leader you'll inspire many people to reach for their goals, but it starts with you. A goal you feel passionate about is the first step toward becoming an elite leader. You can always learn skills. The fire that will take you to the top comes from within.

WHEN THE FIRE GOES OUT

A few years ago, the owner of a direct selling company contacted me with a problem. His business had leveled off, and he invited me to his annual Leadership Retreat to remotivate his leaders.

Because the retreat was at an exotic destination I was excited to go, and I was even more excited when I arrived. One of the benefits of a direct selling business is visiting stunning locations, and the retreat was held in a luxury resort.

When we got down to business I asked all the leaders to share their goals for the year ahead. Most of the goals seemed uninspiring, and many of the leaders struggled to come up with any real goal. Over and over they repeated the same goal: "My goal is to help my team grow."

Helping others grow is not a goal. It's a strategy. Helping others achieve their goals is how we achieve our goals. We get what we want by helping others get what they want.

Everyone listened politely as each leader took her turn to speak. There was little of the energy and excitement that's the norm in a room of direct sellers.

I invited the most senior leader to share her goal, hoping she would step up and set an example. But her only response was to wave toward the others and say, "My only goal is to help all of you. That's what I'm here to learn."

Problem identified. This top leader's fire was extinguished, and her lack of inspiration was influencing the entire leadership group. No wonder the company was flatlining.

I knew what she was earning. The luxury car parked in front of the hotel had her name on its plates, and she was traveling the world on company-paid vacations. This leader was enjoying all the rewards that go with being the highest-paid leader in the company. But she had lost her fire.

When I asked for a personal goal she repeated the same message: "I honestly have everything I want. My goal is helping my leaders grow."

Somehow I had to dismantle the blockade of indifference that was choking the life out of the company. I tried coaxing her to share something a little more personal. After some thought, the best she could come up with was, "I need to do something about our backyard."

It didn't sound inspiring, but it was all I had to work with so I seized on it. "What will you do?"

"Well, we have a ranch-style house that's surrounded by woods."

One of her leaders chipped in, "It's amazing," and everyone agreed.

This leader had all the tangible rewards that money can buy. But we were still going nowhere fast.

"Tell me about your yard," I invited.

"We need to do some landscaping."

"Have you thought about what you'll do?"

She shrugged. "I guess I would like to make the patio area bigger. Maybe extend it the entire length of the house."

We were starting to make progress.

"Sounds great," I encouraged.

That's when I saw the first flicker of light in her eyes. "What I'd really like to do is replace all the windows with French doors so we could walk out onto the patio from any room in the house."

I was starting to picture the patio. "That would be fabulous," I said. Who wouldn't want to step outdoors onto a sunny patio from any room in the house?

The flicker in her eyes sparked as her goal took shape.

"And I want an outdoor kitchen—the full works. A barbecue, and a fire pit so we could entertain all year . . ."

The spark was becoming a flame. "And a huge countertop so we could prepare everything outdoors."

The atmosphere in the room was heating up. Now there was no stopping her.

"And a pizza oven. If we had a pizza oven we could hold pizza parties."

I could feel it. Everyone could feel it. Smoldering embers, the aroma of baking pizza, good times . . .

"We could hold our team meetings outside."

The room was on fire. Everyone was transported to the patio and everyone was inspired.

We were establishing the first rule of direct selling leadership: To be an inspiring leader, you must be inspired.

We should always be grateful for what we have, but leaders can never become complacent. When you're excited by your goals, your excitement fuels the fire in others. Leaders are inspiring because they're inspired!

Once we unlocked the gate, the goals started to flow. Every leader wanted another chance to share her goal. Some made us sad. We learned about a family in debt, a husband desperate to quit his job. Some made us laugh. A guilt-free shopping spree!

It was emotional and exciting, and it set the scene for the training that followed. My goal that weekend was to restart the company's growth, and my reward was receiving feedback that the company was back on the move.

One of your greatest joys will be helping others set and achieve their goals, but you can never lose your passion for setting and achieving your own.

SEVEN STEPS TO FINDING THE RIGHT GOAL

These steps will help you find a goal worthy of the time and energy you'll put into achieving it.

Step One

Choose a goal that makes your heart leap. Small goals will not inspire either you or the people looking to you for inspiration. If you don't feel an immediate, emotional reaction to the goal you've chosen, dig deeper until you find one that does light your fire.

Step Two

If your goal doesn't immediately come to mind, these questions will help you find it:

- ★ *If I could make one personal wish come true, what would it be?*
- ★ *How different would my life be if I had no credit card debt?*
- ★ *Am I driving the car I deserve or the car I can afford?*
- ★ *If I had $10,000 in the bank today, what would I buy with it?*
- ★ *If I won a vacation anywhere in the world, where would I go?*
- ★ *How would it feel to stop renting and own my own home?*
- ★ *If I could transform one room in my house, which room would it be?*
- ★ *Am I happy in my job, or is it time I quit working to make other people rich?*
- ★ *If I could make one family dream come true, what would it be?*
- ★ *What difference would an extra $1,000 a week income make to my life?*

Step Three

Don't confuse goals with strategies. Promoting to a higher level in the compensation plan is a strategy that will help you achieve your goal. Think a step further to how the income and rewards you gain from your new status will impact your life. What will you do with the extra income?

★ Start saving for a down payment on your new home?
★ Give your child the gift of a debt-free college education?
★ Remodel your home?
★ Buy a rental property?
★ Bolster your retirement funds?

When everyone in your organization has a goal they are passionate about, your business will fire on all cylinders. The most effective way to encourage them to share their goals with you is to share yours with them. Imagine sitting across the table from a prospect or a team member and sharing your goal to become a sales leader or director . . . status levels and titles are meaningless to someone who has yet to learn how the compensation plan works. But everyone can relate to taking a family vacation, paying for a child's music lessons, quitting a day job, or saving to start a family.

Step Four

Adopt this rule: one goal, one year, one step at a time. No matter how many goals you can think of, choose only one to pursue. A goal is your compass. It points you in the right direction and keeps you from straying off course. If you head for two destinations, your energies will be scattered and you'll be lucky to reach either of them.

If you're struggling to choose one goal over another, maybe neither of them is important enough to take center stage in your plans. Find the one that will give you the greatest sense of accomplishment by running them through these tests:

The thrill test: Which one will give you the most
satisfaction when you achieve it? Which one makes
your heart beat faster? Which one makes your eyes
shine brighter?

The logic test: Which goal makes more sense? If one of
your goals is to reduce debt but you're tempted to
splurge on a new spring wardrobe, it should be clear
which one to aim for first. By reducing your debt
you'll have more cash for a shopping spree next spring.
But if you can't stop thinking about those clothes,
go for it. If your heart is not in your goal, it's the
wrong goal.

The urgency test: Is there an opportunity you can't afford
to pass up? If your company announces an incentive
trip to a destination you've always wanted to visit,
seize the moment.

Step Five

Be true to yourself. I spend much of my time speaking at conven-
tions and I love it when people share their goals with me. When
one successful leader approached me and said, "I don't have a goal,"
I suspected she was simply reluctant to share it.

She was on a rapid rise up her company's plan so I challenged
her: "With the growth you're accomplishing, I know you must have
a goal."

She answered, "I guess I'm embarrassed about my goal."

When I coaxed her into sharing her goal it did not surprise me.

"I want to be number one in my company. I'm a little embarrassed to admit that."

Goals are deeply personal. If stepping on stage to the applause
of your peers as you take the winner's trophy drives you, make it
your goal. A desire for recognition drives many superachievers. I'm
sure that leader will achieve the recognition she dreams about.

Step Six

Picture yourself achieving your goal. How will you feel when it becomes a reality? Sharing your goal with the people you care about will keep your adrenaline pumping.

Every part of my life has been, and continues to be, achieved one goal at a time. My goal for my first year in business was to earn enough to pay the bills. Once that was accomplished I set my sights on a new car. Moving to a better neighborhood. Family vacations. Sending my children to schools where they would have the best chance of success. Although the goalposts keep shifting, I cannot imagine living my life without goals. They have taken me through bad times and good, failures and successes, disappointments and triumphs.

When we know what we want, we make things happen. When we don't know what we want, we run the risk of a lifetime spent waiting for something to happen.

Step Seven

Before you commit to your goal, make sure you pass it through these reality checks:

> *Is this goal realistic in light of my present circumstances?*
> Reaching beyond our comfort zone is what
> personal growth is all about, but a goal will be
> counterproductive if it's too far out of your reach.
> *Am I prepared to put the time and effort into achieving my
> goal?* It's not enough to want it. You have to be willing
> to work for it.

As your business grows so will your goals. You'll be exposed to new people and experiences. As your horizons expand you'll almost certainly find yourself setting goals that were off your radar when you started out. Your circumstances may change in ways you could never predict. It's the unpredictability of life that makes it exciting.

But there will never be a time when you can run your business on autopilot. By knowing what you want, and pursuing it with relentless enthusiasm, you'll inspire others to do the same. When you achieve your goal you'll become a living example that success in direct selling is believable and achievable.

CHAPTER TWO

Commit to Success

Don't make hope your business plan.
—MARY CHRISTENSEN

There's no halfway when it comes to succeeding in business. You either want it or you don't. Elite leaders don't embrace half measures and they don't make hope their business plan. They succeed on purpose.

As an independent contractor, you own your business, and that gives you ownership of the choices you make. Start by choosing the corporation you partner with. The closer the fit between you and the corporation, the higher your income potential will be, so make sure you're excited about its plan, products, and people.

THE PLAN

Partner with a corporation that offers a tiered (multilevel) compensation plan. Multilevel plans reward you for introducing others to the business and giving them training and support to grow their businesses. Most companies call it duplication, but I call it paying it forward. You'll generate your income by learning how to grow your business and teaching others to do the same.

Compensation plans may differ in the details, but all reward results in these five areas:

1. The number of people you introduce into your organization
2. The total volume of sales those people produce
3. How long they stay active in your organization
4. How many of them climb the compensation plan ladder
5. How high they climb up the compensation plan ladder

Make the compensation plan your blueprint for success. It clearly maps out the rewards you'll enjoy at each level and what you must do to get there.

You can create fire by focusing the rays of the sun onto paper through a lens. It's the intense focus of heat that creates the fire, and the technique requires a steady hand. If you lose concentration and your hand wavers, you won't make fire. It's the same in business. If you focus your time, energy, and resources on the key actions, you'll be rewarded by results. If your attention wavers, your efforts will go to waste. The sharper your focus, the higher your income will be.

THE PRODUCTS

Your status, income, and rewards will be determined by the total sales your business generates, so choose a corporation that has products you believe in.

Being your own best customer will give you credibility when you share your products with others. Building a business around a product that works for you, whether it's skincare, clothes, cookware, or nutritional supplements, is a smart move, as is turning a passion for fashion, jewelry, entertaining, baking, decorating, card making, scrapbooking, or preserving the environment into a profitable business.

THE PEOPLE

You're in the people business. Being in business with people you like, trust, and respect makes sense on both a personal and professional level.

When you love what you do, and the people you work with, your business becomes less like work and more of a lifestyle choice.

Finding the right people for your business is not as simple as asking everybody you know if they want to participate, although you probably already know many people who will be excellent partners. You need people who will commit fully to the business, who will become just as excited as you about the plan and the products.

NEVER LOSE SIGHT OF YOUR GOAL

Apart from choosing your corporate partner, the most powerful choice you'll make is committing to your business. A commitment is a promise that you'll achieve your goal without these self-defeating conditions attached:

> *I will give it my best shot.*
> *I will do it if I can find the right people.*
> *I will do it if the economy picks up.*
> *I will do it when the company changes its policies.*

Our power comes from within. You can refuse to let forces outside your control determine your destiny. You can refuse to be swayed by stories of doom and gloom, and you can refuse to give up on your dreams, no matter what's happening with the economy, or what challenges you're facing personally.

While most people wait for something to happen, you can make things happen. While others wait for things to get better, you can make yourself better.

You'll make mistakes. If you don't, you're not trying hard enough.

You'll face challenges. If you don't, you're playing in the sandbox.

Growing a business takes determination, discipline, and drive. It doesn't matter how many mistakes you make or missteps you take. If you commit to your goal you'll find a way to reach it.

Before starting this book, I fulfilled a lifetime dream of going on safari in East Africa. Although it had always been one of my goals, it never made it to the top of the list. Now it was the goal.

I especially wanted to experience the annual migration, when herds of wildebeest and zebra move between the Serengeti in Tanzania and the Masai Mara in Kenya. Such a massive movement of animals creates a spectacular sight, especially when they cross the murky Mara River.

My husband, friends, and I arrived in Africa equipped and eager to experience one of the most dramatic natural phenomena on earth. From hiring experienced guides to camping just ten miles from the river, we did everything we could to give ourselves the best chance of success.

Witnessing a river crossing is as unpredictable as it is thrilling. Nature has its own plan, and the animals can trek vast distances to the river only to stop before crossing. They're easily startled, and it takes only one front-runner to shy away for the entire herd to follow.

The first morning we struggled to wake after two days of flying and a ten-hour time change. But we hadn't come this far to let jetlag spoil our plans, so we were in the Jeep at dawn. Our reward for a sleep-deprived start, a long bumpy drive on dusty roads, and hours waiting by the river was no crossing.

That night a storm flooded the roads, and the next day we had to follow a more circuitous route. We endured a bone-jarring ride in the Jeep, only to reach the river after the wildebeest had crossed.

One morning while scanning the area with binoculars we sighted a large herd of animals moving toward the river. We raced in their direction only to watch them veer away from the river.

Every day brought challenges. Strong winds. Thunderstorms. Flies. Dust. A road closed by rangers to protect newborn leopard cubs. A sleepy lion that refused to move off the path.

Every journey brought distractions. We encountered more wildlife than we dared hope for. A lonely baboon trying to locate his lost family by climbing to the top of a tree. Playful lion cubs. Skulking hyenas. Magnificent birds of prey strutting inches from our Jeep.

Every day brought new drama as life and death exchanges between predators and their prey played out before our eyes.

Many times we left the path to follow possible sightings of rare cheetahs and leopards and to visit primitive tribal villages.

Twice our courage was tested. When a herd of territorial elephants waded into a stream we were crossing, we quickly gave way. When a black rhino lumbered toward our Jeep we reversed quickly to avoid a showdown.

But we never lost sight of our goal.

One day our spirits lifted at the sight of a thousand wildebeest congregating beside the river. Our anticipation grew as they began moving swiftly toward the bank. But just as they were about to plunge into the water, another Jeep drove too close and spooked the whole herd. Crossing abandoned. Another day the snout of a crocodile rising above the water caused the animals to turn back in panic.

It took many pilgrimages to the river before we captured the spectacular sight of thousands of wildebeest plunging en masse into the river and swimming frantically to the other side. It was all worth it!

Whatever your goal, accept the roadblocks and detours you encounter along the way. Realize that the best-laid plans can fall apart due to circumstances beyond your control. The green light is not always going to be shining in your direction. A commitment means embracing these principles:

> *I want it, I deserve it, I can do it, and I will do it.*
> *If it's not working for me, it is because I'm not doing enough, or*
>   *I'm doing the wrong things.*
> *I will keep working and I will keep learning until I achieve my*
>   *goal.*
> *I cannot fail if I do not quit before I succeed.*

Whether you work part-time, full-time, or in your spare time is up to you. You can combine your direct selling business with a regular job, raising a family, or caring for a loved one.

If you expect a fantasy world where nothing goes wrong, you set yourself up for disappointment. If you commit to achieving your goals on Planet Reality, where even the best plans come unstuck, you'll welcome challenges as part of the journey. When you hit speed bumps, you'll either find a way to remove them or swerve around them, or you'll back up and find another route.

You cannot control what happens along the way, but you can control how you deal with what happens, and you can control your commitment to reaching your destination. Without commitment, goals become little more than pipe dreams.

CHAPTER THREE

Eliminate Self-Sabotage

Stop overestimating the challenge and underestimating yourself.
—Mary Christensen

It's not enough to believe in your products, your company, and the business. You have to believe in yourself.

Every skill you need to be an elite leader is written into your DNA. By strengthening your natural abilities and eliminating self-defeating beliefs and behaviors you'll achieve all the success you dream about. Self-doubt is the single greatest barrier you must cross to earn the highest income. Self-doubt leads to self-sabotage. Sabotage comes in many guises, but they all have the same destructive effect on your business.

In this chapter I'll explore the most common ways we sabotage ourselves. If you make it to the end of the chapter without saying, *That's me!* or *That's what I do!* you already have the personal mastery to succeed. Use what you learn to help others overcome their demons.

ONE: UNDERESTIMATING YOURSELF

If you don't believe you deserve to succeed, you'll find a thousand reasons why you can't.

I'm too new.
I'm too young (old, busy, shy).
I dislike my job but the salary (health plan) is too good
   to give up.
I'm not confident (smart) enough.
I don't want to be seen as taking advantage of others.
My kids are too young (involved in sports).
My job (volunteer work) is too demanding.
I don't have the experience (time, confidence).
I'm only in it for the products.
I'm not educated enough.
I'm too qualified.
It's not what I want.

Thinking this way opens the door for failure to breeze right in. If you're looking for excuses you'll find them everywhere. But you can't make excuses and money at the same time.

I have always dreamed big dreams, but growing up with an alcoholic father who took out his anger at the world on his kids hadn't instilled me with enough confidence to pursue them. I married young, and for all the wrong reasons. You can imagine how well that worked out.

Becoming the key financial provider for my family was the wake-up call I needed to start taking responsibility for my future. And that's when I discovered it took courage, not confidence, to take control of your life.

The first step was giving myself permission to succeed. Although I made many mistakes and took many missteps as I grew my business, I discovered if I was willing to work and willing to learn, nothing could hold me back. I raised my expectations and stopped embracing my tough past as a trophy to victimhood. I saw instead that it had given me the gifts of determination, self-reliance, empathy, and understanding.

It takes courage to push against the emotional barriers that hold others back. Maybe you have personal challenges to deal with. Maybe you've pursued a career that was determined by the expectations of others. Maybe none of your family members has risen above their circumstances. Maybe none of your friends has moved beyond their comfort zone. Maybe you've played it safe all your life. That was then. This is now.

It takes courage to change the path you're on in life. Regardless of how you arrived at this point, if you're on the wrong path, it's time to find a better one. And the time to start is now.

This business expanded my life beyond perimeters I could ever imagine. Not just in financial terms, but also in personal growth and the example of independence and personal power I set for my family. When you give yourself permission to succeed, it will do the same for you.

TWO: OVERTHINKING THE CHALLENGE

When you overthink the challenge involved in growing your business, you risk it becoming a self-fulfilling prophecy. There are no guarantees in life, but worrying about what may go wrong is a waste of the energy you need to propel yourself forward.

There's a difference between facts and feelings, and by confusing the two you allow fear to determine your path in life. Mark Twain once famously admitted, *"I've been through some terrible times in my life, some of which actually happened."*

Fear is paralyzing. It can keep you trapped in a job that gives you no satisfaction, and prevent your moving on from pursuits that are past their use-by date. It can allow you to be swayed by the opinions and expectations of others, and tempt you to stay cocooned in your comfort zone. Courage gives you the power to pursue the life you deserve.

I have this quote from Brian Andreas on my wall: *"Most people don't know that there are angels whose job is to make sure we don't get too comfortable and fall asleep and miss our life."* It reminds me every day that challenges are a catalyst for growth. If you don't keep testing yourself, how can you ever reach your true potential in life? How will you ever know what it is?

Millions of entrepreneurs start a business with a passion that withers on the vine when the going gets tough. The path to the elite levels of the compensation plan is littered with aspiring leaders who fell by the wayside after discovering that enthusiasm is a great business starter but not enough to sustain success long-term. The qualities that set the doers apart from the dreamers are determination, discipline, and drive.

Many great things have been created from imperfection. The great sculptor Michelangelo carved his perfect sculpture of David from marble that was full of flaws. His quote *"I saw the angel in the marble and carved until I set him free"* should inspire all of us to chip away at the beliefs and behaviors that keep us from becoming the person we aspire to be.

You have the freedom to choose your thoughts, and that's where your power lies. Think of how much you have to lose before you choose to dwell on negativity.

* ★ *What if you had what it takes to live an amazing life but you gave up without giving it your best shot?*
* ★ *What if you wasted the potential you were born with because you let fear paralyze you?*
* ★ *What if hell was discovering what you could have done with your life?*

Your greatest fear should not be the obstacles you face. Your greatest fear should be that one day you'll look back with regret at all the opportunities you wasted in life because you let fear beat you down.

Economies go in cycles. We can all expect to experience good and bad economic times. But people succeed in good times and people succeed in bad times. What sets achievers apart is that a challenge makes them, while most people let challenges break them. Instead of wallowing in worry, achievers get on with the job.

THREE: OVERLOADING YOURSELF

The number of hours you invest in your business will determine how quickly you grow. One of the surest ways to sabotage yourself is to fill your days with busywork. Successful leaders tackle high-priority tasks first. They don't push paper around a desk or play games on their computer when they could be working the front line of their businesses.

Time is your most precious resource, and if you're drowning in a quagmire of minutiae, it's time to rethink your priorities in life. If you're serious about building your business, start trimming or eliminating time-wasting activities:

- ★ Make lists so you know exactly what you have to do each day and check off each item as you complete it.
- ★ Create a new list each night so you can start fresh the next morning.
- ★ Highlight the most productive tasks and tackle them first.
- ★ Finish what you start before moving to the next task.
- ★ Don't be a hoarder or a stacker. Deal with it, delegate it, or discard it.
- ★ Stop obsessively checking your e-mails and limit your time on Facebook.
- ★ Send a text instead of an e-mail. Your message will transmit faster, and you can almost guarantee it will be read instantly.

★ Scan and save documents on your PC, where you can file and retrieve them easily.

★ Download training modules and listen as you exercise, run errands, drive, or walk the dog.

★ Keep your workspace organized. If it's a multipurpose area, a couple of plastic filing bins will work effectively.

Don't become so obsessed with your phone that it becomes a liability:

★ Ditch your landline and go mobile.

★ Control incoming calls by letting people know the best times to call.

★ Use caller ID so you can identify low- and high-priority calls.

★ Control outgoing calls by making important calls when your energy level is high and routine calls when you're less tempted to chat.

★ Work out what you want to say before you pick up the phone.

★ Respect those you're calling by asking, *Is this a convenient time for you?*

★ End a call that's dragging on by saying, *I'm taking too much of your time. I'll let you go.*

★ Avoid being hijacked by callers who want to chat by saying:

It's great to hear from you. What can I help you with today?
It's good to hear your voice. I'm on a bit of a deadline right now. Can I call you later?
Thank you for calling. Is it possible this can wait until next week?
I appreciate your call. I know you're busy, so let's try to handle this by e-mail.

Running your personal life efficiently is an effective way to create time for your business:

★ Set your alarm fifteen minutes earlier.
★ Buy supplies in bulk.
★ Set up automatic bill payments.
★ Prepare two meals at once and you'll have one to reheat later in the week.
★ Prepare tomorrow's lunchboxes when you're making tonight's dinner.
★ Record favorite TV programs so you can fast-forward through commercials.
★ Involve family members by asking them each to adopt a job. Sweeten the deal by letting them select a reward to work toward, such as a favorite meal, family outing, extra pocket money, more phone minutes.
★ Hire others to do anything that costs less than you can earn working your business.
★ Add all your birthday, anniversary, and special occasion reminders into your calendar at the start of the year.
★ Practice the word "No" until you can say it without guilt, embarrassment, or fear.
★ Deal with people who think working from home is an invitation to take time off anytime you want, by saying, *Thanks for thinking of me but I can't take the time off work.*
★ If they respond, *But I thought you worked for yourself,* or *But you work from home,* say, *I do. That's why I have to be super-disciplined.*

Don't multitask your way to mediocrity. Multitasking is great for day-to-day chores, but it's a poor business strategy. To join the 1 percent of direct sellers who are enjoying the income and rewards that flow at the top of the compensation plan, do what they do, and spend the bulk of your time on activities that generate your income.

FOUR: BEING UNPREPARED

Networking is the life and breath of your business. The more people you meet, the faster your business will grow.

Humans are instinctive networkers. It's natural for us to start and build relationships. Women especially can strike up a conversation, even with a stranger, in seconds. We find it practically impossible to stand beside someone for a few minutes and not start talking (although you'll rarely hear men saying to the person next in line, *I love your shoes* . . .).

However, there's a big "but." If you're not prepared to take advantage of networking opportunities in your community you may as well stay home, watch reruns of *The Biggest Loser*, and eat brownies.

We network to meet people with whom we can share our products, our host opportunities, and our business. The chance to network can arise anywhere, anytime, so make sure you're prepared to seize the moment when it does. Always carry samples, catalogs, and business flyers with you. Enter new contact names and numbers into your phone, or keep blank business cards so you can note a name, e-mail address, or phone number on the spot. The only time it's a good idea to pass out samples or literature to someone without getting that person's contact details for follow-up is . . . *never*!

Keep your networking tools accessible. One successful leader I admire tucks a product catalog under her arm everywhere she goes. She joins the longest line at the checkout and browses her catalog. When someone shows interest, she is ready to share.

Another goes to all of her children's activities, first because she gets to spend more time with them, but second because she's looking for moms just like her to share her business with. She passes out her monthly flyer at the sidelines of her son's ice hockey games as she cheers on his team.

Many successful direct sellers routinely hand out "introductory special" or "thank-you offer" cards to the people they meet while out shopping or running errands.

A medical practitioner I admire has flyers promoting his products on his reception desk, and copies of relevant articles in his patient waiting area. He refreshes his messages according to the season, from safeguarding against winter colds to being sun-safe in summer. There's no pressure, just a desire to help his patients maintain good health. Many times the flyers have opened the door to a conversation that leads to a new customer or recruit.

In my book *Be a Party Plan Superstar* I recommend that party planners take at least three host packs and three business packs to every party, and position them prominently amongst their product display. Every group presentation is a golden opportunity to build your contacts. If your focus is top-heavy on products, it will be at the expense of booking and business opportunities.

To avoid a slow, uncertain climb to the top of your compensation plan, give equal thought time, show time, and talk time to the products, bookings, and the business. Sales generate your income for today, bookings generate your income for tomorrow, and recruiting generates your income forever.

So much of this business is about being in the right place at the right time when the right people come along, but if you're not ready to act when that happens, you can be sure someone else will seize the opportunity you squandered.

FIVE: PROCRASTINATING

Procrastination is perhaps the most destructive form of self-sabotage of all. What can be any more convenient excuses than these and others like them?

I'll do it tomorrow (next week, next year).
I'll have more time when the holidays are over.
I'll wait for the new catalog.
I'll complete my degree first.
I'll start when the kids are back in school.
I'll master the product knowledge first.
I'll start when it stops snowing.

Life is not a dress rehearsal, and every day you let slip by is a day wasted. None of us can ever know what tomorrow will bring, and the smallest step you take today will count more than the thousand giant strides you intend to take tomorrow.

When you want it badly enough you'll find a way to work around whatever circumstances or challenges you have today. You'll pick up the phone when you feel like it and, more important, even when you don't. You'll find time every day to grow your business because you know there will never be the "perfect" time.

Ultimately, what will set you apart from the pack is knowing your strengths and your shortcomings while refusing to let self-doubt steal your dreams. What will set you apart is a willingness to work around personal and business challenges, and see mistakes as a lesson, not a setback. When something is not working, you'll change it and change it fast.

When you choose not to make failure an option you'll find a way to deal with every roadblock, real or perceived, that you confront.

CHAPTER FOUR

Share Your Story

There's no better way to position your products, business,
and yourself than by sharing your story.
—MARY CHRISTENSEN

All marketers promote their products by telling stories. The difference between the stories direct sellers tell and the ones you see in the media is that ours are not manufactured by an advertising or public relations company. They are real stories told by real people sharing real-life experiences.

But that's where the difference ends. There are billions of products and businesses competing for your customers and prospects. In a crowded marketplace your stories must attract attention, hold interest, and inspire your target audience to do business with you.

Whether you're addressing an audience of one or one thousand, the best stories succeed on three fronts:

1. They connect you with your audience.
2. They communicate your message.
3. They continue on to a "next step."

CONNECT WITH YOUR AUDIENCE

Building rapport with your audience is key to being a persuasive communicator. The more you know about them, the better equipped you'll be to tailor your messages to their interests and experiences. If you don't know whom you're addressing you could be wasting your time and theirs.

We warm to people who are warm toward us. Never start a presentation before you've shown a genuine interest in your prospects and have learned about their lives. It's easy to build rapport in a one-on-one situation, but it will take a little more effort with larger gatherings.

I always mingle with my audiences before I speak. It shows I care about them and it helps me pick up the mood of the event. I start smaller gatherings by inviting guests to introduce themselves.

The simplest way to get to know your audience at larger events is to ask for a show of hands. For example, if you're promoting your business you'll want to know this basic information at least:

* ★ Who works outside the home?
* ★ Who's a stay-at-home parent?
* ★ Who combines the two?

Starting a party by asking, "Who's here because they cannot wait to try our products, and who's here because there's nothing on television?" This question shows you're not taking your guests' attention for granted.

Here are a few more ways to begin a party:

Laughter is the perfect icebreaker, and by showing your
     fun side you're guaranteed a more attentive audience.
Any mom with young children will relate to this
     comment: *You may be wondering if this is my full-time job.*

Actually, my full-time job is being mom to my twin boys, so I call this my sanity job.

Most full-time workers will relate to this comment: *The only time I think about returning to my old job is . . . never!*

People do business with people they like, and as the saying goes . . . *Only fools rush in.* You can never spend too much time building relationships with your future customers, hosts, and prospects.

COMMUNICATE YOUR MESSAGE

Less is most definitely more when it comes to communicating your message. This business is not about finding the right words; it's about finding the right people.

The reason you share your business story is to elicit one of these responses:

I'd love to do something like this.
I wonder if I could do this?
I'm definitely interested in learning more.
This is exactly what I've been looking for.
It's time I quit working for someone else.
I'd love to have my own business.
I wonder how much it costs to start?
Maybe I could do this part-time?
Extra income would be great.
It sounds like a lot of fun.
I'd like to take one of those business flyers.
I wish my partner could hear this.
I hope I get a chance to ask couple of questions.
I wonder if he'll ask me?

An effective way to compile a compelling business story is to use this basic template:

I am . . .
But . . .
And so . . .

Here are some examples:

I am . . . a registered nurse and I love my job.
But . . . I find the shift work quite difficult, especially in
winter.
And so . . . I'm working toward making this my full-time job.

I am . . . a doctor.
But . . . so many of my patients could avoid a visit to my offices
if they took better care of themselves.
And so . . . I started my nutritional business to help my patients
stay healthy. It's much more rewarding than waiting for my
patients to get sick before they seek my advice.

I am . . . a teacher.
But . . . because I was the last one to be hired I will be the first
to go if the school budget is cut. It's stressful not knowing if I
have a job each year.
And so . . . I have decided to work for myself. I'm just starting
out, but I'm having so much fun it hardly feels like work,
and the support I get from the company is amazing.

I am . . . a stay-at-home mom and I'm lucky my husband has a
good job.
But . . . it seems everything he earns gets eaten up by bills.
And so . . . this business pays for the extras we enjoy as a

family. This year I'm working toward a family trip to Disneyland.

If you're a full-time direct seller, a more appropriate template is:

I was . . .
But . . .
And so . . .

I was . . . an engineer for a construction firm.
But . . . when the economy slowed I lost my job.
And so . . . I started my own business. After six months my only regret is I didn't do it sooner. What felt like a disaster when it happened turned out to be a blessing. I used to spend two hours a day commuting. Now my commute is two minutes and I can spend that time with my wife and kids.

I was . . . in business for myself. I owned a hair salon.
But . . . it was hard going it alone. I was always fretting about whether I could find the right staff, or pay the bills. Then my landlord raised my rent.
And so . . . I decided to look for a business where I had more control and more freedom. And I found it!

You will notice that every story is one of personal growth. Don't be afraid to show vulnerability. We all are inspired by people who rise from adversity and triumph over challenges.

The wider you cast your net, the more people will find your offer appealing. By keeping your personal testimony brief you will allow time to reach out to prospects with different ambitions, experiences, and circumstances.

Let's say you're a home-based entrepreneur with a party plan business and your guests are an equal mix of stay-at-home moms and workers. If your story focuses solely on the benefits of combining work and family, you effectively rule out half your prospects.

Here's an example of how you can embrace both groups:

> Some of you may be wondering if this is my real job. Actually my real job is being mom to three girls. But before I started my family I was a lawyer, and as much as I love being a stay-at-home mom I found it hard giving up my independence. My business gives me the best of both worlds. I can be there for my girls and also have some valuable "me" time. Plus, the extra income makes a huge difference to our family.
>
> What's exciting is my team members are all so different. Some are working full-time jobs and doing this for extra cash. Others are building businesses so they can quit their day jobs. We complement each other, as everyone brings different skills and perspectives to the business.

In this example it took only thirty seconds to create a picture of how the business fits a stay-at-home mom and a full-time worker. It also plants seeds for a significant career move.

Your business will be built one person at a time and the broader your story, the more likely you'll hear the magic response: *This sounds like my dream job.*

The same principles apply to making a product presentation. The more people you appeal to, the more sales you'll make. There will most likely be people in your audience who will buy and those who may buy if you position your products in a way they can relate to.

Let's imagine you're promoting quality cookware to a mixed audience. Anyone who loves to cook will automatically appreciate having the best cookware. Their attention is guaranteed, but you'll make more sales if you broaden your message to include people who are less passionate about spending time in the kitchen.

You may think I do this because I love to cook. But actually I do this because I have to cook. I have five kids and the closest store is ten miles away. I really appreciate having the best cookware because it makes my life easier. When I bought my first set of pans the difference was so incredible all I could think of was, how come it took me so long? Plus, our oven-to-table dishes save me so much time when it comes to washing up. I also love that they come with airtight lids so I can pop leftovers straight into the fridge.

If you're selling products your customer can experience, work that advantage. When they can taste-test the foods, try on the clothes and accessories, enjoy the fragrance of candles, or visualize decorative items in their home, your customers' senses will do your work for you.

For many products, such as skincare and nutritional supplements, you're essentially selling a promise. It's not enough to talk about the difference the products make in your life. Your stories have to create a picture of what your products will do for your audience.

I'll use skincare products as an example. Your first goal is to inspire your customers to start taking better care of their skin by presenting a persuasive argument about aging. For example:

★ *Eighty percent of skin aging is premature and preventable.*
★ *The sun's rays accelerate aging as much as eight times. That means for every hour you spend in the sun, your skin ages a day.*
★ *None of us, ten years from now, will regret taking care of our skin today.*

Your next goal is to prime each customer for action by inspiring one of these responses:

I need everything!
I'm definitely placing an order.

*I'll buy as much as I can afford . . . and I must find out more
    about the host program.*

The more compelling your message is, the higher your sales will be. Remember, you're not selling formulas; you're selling youthful, vibrant skin.

Your message will be more persuasive if you reinforce the results your customer will experience within your product story:

I was skeptical at first, but the difference was truly amazing.
I love the way this cleanser melts into my skin.
*What I love most about this night cream is how my skin feels in
    the morning.*
This shower gel is one luxury you won't want to give up.
This eye cream is addictive.
Within days your skin is going to look fresher, brighter, younger.
Everyone reorders this lotion.
The results will speak for themselves.
*I know you're going to tell me this is the best skincare you have
    ever used.*
*For the cost of an hour at the spa, you could treat your skin to
    these beautiful products for a month.*

If you're marketing nutritional supplements your message must appeal to at least three different audiences: those who want to attain good health, those who want to regain good health, and those who want to maintain good health.

I have attended many events at which a distributor has shared a lengthy personal testimony about the difference a nutritional product has made on his or her health without reaching out to a broader audience. The reality is most of us have short attention spans when it comes to other people's health issues, and the gamble you take when you overemphasize your own experiences is that you'll lose the attention of audience members who are don't have health issues and are interested only in staying healthy.

Here is an example of how you can broaden your message but still incorporate your own story:

> I always took my health for granted, and it took a major illness to give me the wake-up call I needed to start taking better care of myself. I truly believe these supplements gave me a second chance, but I think the message applies to all of us. Life is too short to take risks with your health.
>
> It's hard to eat the right foods when you're busy and if you're eating on the run, as most of us are these days, it makes sense to take supplements. I like to think of it as health insurance. None of us, ten years from now, will regret taking care of our health today.

When your message packs a punch you don't need to dwell on the details. When your message embraces everyone in your audience you'll keep their attention. When a direct seller asks me how to deal with inattentive guests who chat while they're presenting, all I can say is, "Lighten up a little. You're probably boring them."

Never take your audience for granted. They have given you their time, but you have to earn their attention. If you're not an interesting storyteller, they'll flick their mental "off" switch and you'll be addressing an audience of none.

CONTINUE ON TO A "NEXT STEP"

It's not enough to open your mouth and let the words spill out. You have to invite interested prospects to take a next step. That won't happen if you dominate the conversation. By involving your audience in the presentation, you'll know who is responding to your stories.

You can take the guesswork out of the process by asking interesting questions. Interesting questions invite interesting answers that reveal the personalities in your audience. By tailoring your questions to your products, you'll identify who has a need or desire to buy them. For example:

* *If you could change one thing about your skin, what would it be?*
* *If you could improve one thing about your diet, what would it be?*
* *If you could change one thing about your health, what would it be?*
* *If you could remodel one room in your home, which room would it be?*
* *If you were asked to share one recipe with a friend, which one would it be?*

These questions will identify a need or desire for your business opportunity:

* *Who dreams of quitting their day job?*
* *Who wants a lifestyle that's bigger than their paycheck?*
* *What difference would an extra $200 a week make to your life?*
* *If you could change one thing about your job, what's the first thing you would do?*

You'll notice the questions are focused. Focused questions are a shortcut to great feedback and reduce the risk of getting a rambling answer that goes nowhere.

Interesting answers will help clarify the next step you'll invite a prospect to take:

★ Placing an order
★ Signing up for auto-ship
★ Booking a presentation or consultation
★ Meeting with you to talk about the business
★ Coming to a special business event
★ Taking home a host or business pack
★ Signing on the spot

Always end your presentation by asking for the order. If you don't offer a next step, you won't close the sale.

CHAPTER FIVE

Become a Persuasive Communicator

You can't learn to speak up sitting down.
—MARY CHRISTENSEN

Tens of thousands of direct sellers start businesses every day, but fewer than 1 percent make it to the top of the plan. To be one of the 1 percent you have to master the attitudes and skills of the 1 percent.

Lifting your game as a communicator will positively impact the outcome of your business at every level:

★ Marketing your products effectively will lead to more and larger orders.
★ Servicing your customers regularly will generate repeat business, as well as referrals, bookings, and sponsoring leads.
★ Presenting your host rewards enthusiastically will attract more bookings.
★ Sharing your business persuasively will lead to new recruits.

The more effectively you inspire, train, and coach your recruits, the higher your sales, bookings, recruiting, and leader promotions will be.

In the last chapter I looked at how to create persuasive product and business stories. In this chapter I will share my best tips for making compelling communications to a larger audience. Don't let fear stop you from speaking out. Most of us feel overwhelmed at the thought of speaking in public. We're all a little in awe of someone who can hold an audience spellbound with a presentation that appears as effortless as it is captivating. But in all probability years of practice preceded the impressive performance. Most of us have to work hard at perfecting our communication skills, and the more ambitious you are, the more time and effort you should invest.

I was a teacher before I started my direct selling business, and I hoped my experience in front of a classroom would transfer to my new endeavor. But that was not the case. I was so nervous when I stood up to speak that my knees shook. I was often dumbstruck by the sea of faces looking back at me.

I will never forget my first time behind a microphone. As I started to speak a loud thumping resonated through the room. I could see the audience was confused by the noise, but I knew exactly what it was. My heart was beating so loudly you could hear it through the sound system. Mortifying.

That's when I knew I had to overcome my fear of speaking before it stopped my business in its tracks. I joined an organization that helped people like me conquer the panic we felt at being in the spotlight. I worked on eliminating my bad habits and learned to separate the following facts from fiction about communicating:.

Fiction: Communication is about sharing information.
Fact: Many direct sellers make the mistake of thinking the more information they share, the more their audiences will be persuaded. But most of us can absorb information only in small doses. Great communicators focus more on making an impact than on sharing information. If you engage your audience emotionally as well as logically, they'll respond to you and your presentation.

Fiction: Communication is about finding the right words.

Fact: Words are not your friend. Compelling communicators are more concerned about gathering information than giving it. Learn as much as you can about your audience. When you get to know the people you're talking to you can tailor your presentations to their needs, interests, and circumstances.

Fiction: The best communicators have a dynamic style.

Fact: You can be equally effective whether you're a subtle presenter or a forceful one. What does matter is that you're genuine. Substance will always win over style, and sincerity will triumph over spin. One of my favorite quotes, *"Be yourself. Everyone else is already taken,"* sums it up perfectly. Don't compare yourself to others. Work to your own strengths.

Fiction: It takes confidence to be an effective communicator.

Fact: Respecting your audience is far more important than confidence. We've all suffered through excruciatingly bad presentations delivered by speakers whose confidence is exceeded only by their tediousness. The more time you spend working on the quality of your message the less time you'll have to worry about your insecurities.

Fiction: It's a good idea to tell your audience how nervous you are.

Fact: Your audiences want to like you and they want you to entertain and enlighten them. If you start talking about how nervous you are they'll start feeling sorry for you instead of intrigued about what you have to say. A simple way to calm yourself is to inhale deeply and exhale slowly several times before you start speaking. At the very least it will distract you from focusing on your nerves. Pre-presentation jitters are usually a sign that you want to do a good job, but when you appear relaxed your audience will relax.

Fiction: Public speaking skills are becoming redundant now that we have technology to do our communicating for us.

Fact: Don't become so bewitched by e-tools that you ignore the magic of meeting in person. Technology makes it easier to talk to your audience, but when you're face-to-face you're talking *with* your audience.

PRACTICE MAKES PERFECT

As your business grows you'll have increasing opportunities to speak in front of a larger audience. Seek out and accept every speaking invitation and opportunity you can. You can't learn to speak up sitting down.

The experience will be less nerve-wracking if you adopt the three keys to great communications:

1. Prepare
2. Practice
3. Polish

Even the most accomplished performers rehearse their lines. If you've seen an actor stumble after being caught off guard during an interview you'll know how lack of preparation leads to a poor performance. If you're a confident communicator, there's still no excuse for being ill prepared. Your audience deserves better.

Shine when it's your time in the spotlight by following ten proven steps to a winning presentation.

Step One

The place to start preparing your presentation is at the end of it. Ask yourself, *What do I want my audience to think, feel, and do when I have finished speaking?* Whether your goal is to inspire a group of prospects to start a business, encourage your recruits to set their sights higher, or motivate your team to aim for a specific incentive, when you know where you're heading you can build your presentation toward your close.

Step Two

Ask yourself, *What information will help my audience change their attitudes and actions?* Use facts sparingly. Customers want solutions to their problems, not explanations about your products. Prospects want to be excited and reassured that they can succeed in their own business, and team members want to believe they'll achieve the exciting incentives your corporation offers. Focus on making an impact on your audience, not broadcasting information.

Step Three

Black and white tells, color sells. Color your presentations with stories, examples, and testimonials. Use anecdotes, quotes, and humor to bring your facts to life. Personal stories are best, but it's okay to import great material from a third party if you convey it well. Avoid worn-out phrases such as "fastest growing" or "best quality," as they're a sign you have little imagination or originality (the word "lazy" also springs to mind). Everyone relates to real-life stories.

Step Four

You have only a few seconds to make a positive impression on your audience, and if you don't win them over in the first few minutes it can be an uphill battle. Design an opening that will attract attention and lead into the body of your presentation. It can range from an interesting story to a powerful statement or thought-provoking question.

I try to keep my openings flexible, so my first comments reflect something that is happening at the event, or flow on from the speaker before me. This helps to build empathy with my audience and shows I'm not a cookie-cutter presenter. However, I always have a back-up opening prepared.

Many times I have been presented with a brilliant opening that I would have missed if my preparation had been too rigid.

Step Five

Your close is your call to action. Without a strong close you have taken your audience on a journey to nowhere. End your presentation with a bang, not a whimper.

Step Six

Editing is every great communicator's secret weapon, and now is the time to eliminate clutter before it drags down your presentation. Look for ways you can make it more powerful. Is one story so strong the other is unnecessary? Have you included too many examples? Do you have a clear opening, an interesting body, and a compelling close?

Most first drafts include material that becomes redundant when the whole presentation is laid out. By eliminating the weaker points you allow stronger points to shine and avoid the risk of speaking beyond your audience's attention span.

Step Seven

When you're happy with your content, draft an outline of key points ready for rehearsing. Many presenters use notes, cue cards, and slides to keep them on track, or as security against stage fright. They can be a great support for beginners, but make sure they're not draining the life out of your presentation. A little spontaneity goes a long way toward winning over an audience. There is nothing more boring than a speech read from notes, and nothing alarms an audience faster than a presenter who steps up to the lectern with a ream of paper or begins a bulky fact-filled PowerPoint presentation.

Using notes for a personal story is a sign of poor preparation. Cramming too much information onto slides no one can read shows a disregard for your audience. Prepare a handout if you have information your audience should keep, but don't become one of those dull speakers who use statistics and "stuff" to look important. No one will be fooled.

The reason I don't use notes is that I want to be able to respond to my audiences' reactions, and to take a detour if I feel it is appropriate. I highly recommend that you lose the cue cards as your confidence grows. It takes courage but it's worth it. What helped me make the leap was understanding that my audience would not know if I forgot a point or skipped a story, because they did not know what I had intended in the first place.

Step Eight

The more time you spend polishing them, the brighter your presentations will shine. Shut the door to remove distractions and rehearse in front of an imaginary audience until you're happy with the result. Only the most talented of writers can create written words that mimic the spoken word. By practicing out loud, on your feet, you'll be able to inject your personality into the performance and eliminate imperfections:

★ Does your voice convey enthusiasm and credibility?
★ Do you vary your pace and pitch?
★ Do you talk too fast?
★ Where can you add pauses for effect?
★ Are you trying to cram too much information into too little time?

Use the stopwatch on your smart phone to time your presentation. You'll be forgiven for stopping a little short of your allotted time, but not for exceeding it.

Step Nine

Before you step into the spotlight, picture yourself doing a great job. If you worry about failing on stage and it happens, you've lived the nightmare twice. Your time is better spent on positive imagery. Easier said than done, but the more often you speak the sooner you'll conquer your anxieties.

Step Ten

When it's time to begin, smile, make eye contact, and start talking.

★   ★   ★

The only true measure of an effective presentation is results. After every presentation, take time to review your performance:

* *Did I get the result I wanted?*
* *What did I do well?*
* *Did any part of my speech fall flat?*
* *Was it because my presentation wasn't strong enough or my performance wasn't strong enough?*
* *What can I do better next time?*
* *When will the next time be?*

There are no shortcuts. Prepare, practice, and polish. Prepare, practice, polish.

CHAPTER SIX

Work the Numbers

Believe in everyone, rely on no one.
—MARY CHRISTENSEN

I recently joined a table of trophy winners on Awards Night. As I congratulated the person sitting next to me, I asked, "What made you choose this company?"

Her response? "I always wanted to do this, so I attended every party I was invited to. But no one ever asked me. This was the first company to ask and I jumped at it."

"I wonder why no one asked you?" I said.

She looked a little wistful. "So do I."

She had put herself in opportunity's way many times but no one had cared enough to notice. No doubt her confidence took a hit each time she felt rejected.

There are three lessons to be learned from this story.

★ First, if you don't seize the opportunity someone else will.

★ Second, you must offer the business to everyone, without letting presumption and prejudice get in the way. No one builds a successful business by trying to handpick a team. You'll never know who's interested until you ask, and you'll never know who has potential unless you give them an opportunity to demonstrate it.

★ Third, it's a poignant lesson about rejection. No one likes rejection, but the truth is you reject everyone to whom you fail to offer the opportunity. If you're concerned about the possibility of being rejected, you're focusing on yourself. That means you're focusing on the wrong person.

I wish all the direct sellers who snubbed this wonderful woman could see what they were missing out on. Did their fear of rejection blind them to a hot prospect? Would they have done things differently if they had been able to foresee her turning up at a convention as the star performer with another company and another leader?

The more people you ask, the more will say "yes." Rejection goes with the territory, and if you're not hearing "no" a lot, you're playing it far too safe. Some recruits will come easily, but others will take more effort. Keep an optimistic mindset by remembering that you're not creating a need; you're meeting a need.

With more than a hundred thousand new direct sellers worldwide signing an independent contractor agreement every day, your job is to make sure more of them are signing with you.

That's only the tip of the iceberg. Millions have considered the business but have not followed through, and millions more either haven't heard about direct selling or haven't seriously considered it. The potential is staggering.

KEEP ON SPONSORING

Sponsoring is your route to the elite ranks of direct selling, but you have to be in it to win it. If you genuinely believe in your business you won't hesitate to seek out and invite others to join. This business changed my life, so by offering the business I know I'm paying my prospects a compliment, and doing them a favor.

It starts by putting yourself in the best place to meet people, and that's at parties and presentations. Many leaders tell me they are "burned out" on parties, and others that they feel "above" doing them. As leaders, they feel their focus should shift to helping their teams. There are many reasons why this strategy is flawed, but the major reason is that parties and presentations are where you'll meet your future recruits and leaders.

These perspectives may help you understand the importance of doing parties and presentations no matter how high you are on the leader ladder:

* The more people you meet, the more people you'll sponsor. There are no shortcuts. Talking to people is the only way to generate business.
* Your profit from sales will be anywhere from $100 to $500 per party or presentation. If you do your job right you'll meet your next recruit at the party. Think of it as being paid to recruit. How many entrepreneurs are paid to build their businesses?
* As much effort as you put into attracting your next recruit at the party, it's always going to be a whole lot easier than making cold calls in the morning.
* Your next recruit will have both a chance to see you in action and the benefit of a live demonstration of how the business works.

Sponsoring is being in the right place at the right time when the right person comes along, and there's no downside to maintaining a consistent schedule of parties, presentations, and face-to-face consultations. Offer the business to everyone to the best of your ability and let your prospects decide whether to accept or decline your offer.

One of the greatest advantages of direct selling is how easy it is to join. Naturally we attract a wide range of people. Many join on impulse, and some with short-term goals. A few join to buy the products at wholesale prices, and others are tempted by the contents of the starter kit. Not everyone will have the focus, drive, and discipline needed to succeed.

We all have sponsored people who underestimated the work involved or overestimated the rewards. However, just as we make it easy to start a business, we make it easy to leave. It's most likely that your business will be a revolving door of people coming and going. Industry averages indicate that half of all new recruits will leave within the first three months, and four out of five will be gone by the end of the first year.

This is healthy. Direct selling has an open-door policy for anyone over eighteen years of age, and we are proud of that, especially because departing recruits will most likely leave with more than they put into the business in the first place. When you accept that people will come and go, some will perform a little, some a lot, and some will stall before they reach the starting gate, you'll be sure to introduce a steady flow of new people into your business.

You cannot control what your team members will do. Despite your best efforts they'll do what they want to do. If you're a strong leader they'll stay longer and perform better, but the only security you have is numbers. To keep your business firing on all cylinders, you have to keep fueling it.

Direct selling has always been a numbers game. The more Distributors you have, the greater your chances of finding your future leaders. But there's a catch here too. When your star performers promote to a higher rank, your income will drop until you rebuild your personal group.

MY TOP TEN SPONSORING TIPS

TIP #1: Give Equal Time to Sponsoring
Apply as much focus, time, and energy to sponsoring as you do to selling and scheduling appointments. Practice and teach this basic principle:

Sales are my income for today, scheduling is my income for tomorrow, and sponsoring is my income forever.

Give equal thought time, show time, and talk time to sales, bookings, and the business. What you focus on, your audience will focus on. If you spend 90 percent of your time on sales, and squeeze bookings and sponsoring mentions into the last 10 percent, you'll achieve impressive sales but less-than-impressive bookings and business leads.

Start every day by asking:

What will I do today to generate more sales?
What will I do today to generate more bookings?
What will I do today to generate more business leads?

Before every presentation, affirm your three goals in specific terms. For example:

Tonight I will sell $500, make three bookings, and find two
  business prospects.

Position your business packs prominently. The eye is more powerful than the ear, so place your business materials into bags and top them with tissue for extra visibility. Every time you talk about the business, hold up the bag.

Take a business brochure to every appointment and place it on the table between you and your prospect. Do all you can to leave without it.

When you're out in public, never be caught saying, "I don't have a brochure on me right now."

Spend as much time talking about the business as the products. You won't come across as heavy-handed if you keep your messages fresh and interesting.

Here's how to do it. In a typical presentation you may talk about five to ten different products. Incorporate the business by sandwiching a variety of business commercials between each product. For example, you can include:

★ Your personal story
★ Leading questions
★ Simple games to help you identify your best prospect
★ Information about the business
★ Information about how to get started
★ A show-and-tell to introduce the kit
★ General invitations to join:

> *We're always looking for the right people. If you want to find out more please take one of these business bags home with you. I brought enough for everyone.*
>
> *I mustn't forget to tell you about an event we have coming up. Because everyone seems to be looking for business opportunities right now, and most people like to find out more before they commit, we sponsor a Start Your Own Business Seminar once a month. It only lasts an hour and there's no obligation. If you're interested let me know and I'll make sure you receive an invitation.*

★ Direct invitations to join:

> *Have you ever thought about doing something like this? You're exactly the type of person we are looking for.*
>
> *With your experience, you would be a great asset to our team. We'd love to help you get started.*

If you have the right mindset, you won't let opportunity go to waste. You'll think, show, and talk about the business at every opportunity. If an opportunity doesn't present itself, you'll create one.

For more on how to successfully blend the business into every presentation I highly recommend my book *Be a Party Plan Superstar*. Even if you're not a party planner you'll find a wealth of winning tips inside it. It can be ordered from any online retailer or bookstore.

TIP #2: Create Sparks

Most of your prospects will not be thinking about the business. Your job is to make them think about it. Some will have lukewarm curiosity. Your job is to turn that tepid interest into white-hot desire.

I like to think of it as creating sparks. Everyone has a fire inside, a flame that keeps us alive. But most of us have only the tiny flame of a pilot light. When the right stimulus is applied, it ignites into fire. It happens when you feel passionate about a cause and you're spurred to do something. It happens when you sense danger on the road and spring into evasive action.

This instinctive, emotional response is very powerful. Every decision we make to change our lives starts with a spark that ignites. We do what we are inspired to do, and that includes starting a business.

No matter how powerful your sparks are, they must make a direct hit on a prospect's interests and circumstances to be effective. Make it your goal to strike your prospect with a flash of lightning that triggers one of these responses:

I could do this.
I'd love to do something like this.
Maybe it's time I did something about my job.
This sounds like the perfect job for me.
Sounds like my dream job.
I wonder how much it costs to start?

TIP #3: Get Them to Share Their Gap

What drives us is not what we have, but the gap between what we have and what we want. By encouraging your prospects to share that gap, you're halfway toward closing the deal.

The way to do this is to ask interesting questions. No one gets excited by routine, boring questions, and that's why we respond to such questions on autopilot. Think of how many times you offer an automatic response to everyday questions without engaging your brain:

> *How are you?—Fine, thanks.*
> *Can I help you?—Just looking, thanks.*
> *How's the family?—Great, and yours?*

Interesting questions awaken the senses in a way mundane questions never can. Interesting questions invite interesting answers that reveal interesting information about our prospects, which takes us closer to the sale. Your questions must be appropriate for your audience, of course, but here are some of my favorites:

★ *If you could change one thing about your job, what's the first thing you would do?*
★ *If you had $1,000 in your pocket right now, what would you spend it on?*
★ *If you were given a $100 a week pay raise, what would you do with it?*
★ *How different would your life be if you had no credit card debt?*
★ *If you could take a vacation anywhere in the world, where would you go?*
★ *If you won your dream car in a contest, what would it be?*
★ *If you could make one family dream come true, what would it be?*

★ *If you could make just one personal wish come true, what would it be?*

★ *If you became an instant millionaire, what's the first thing you would do?*

★ *If you could make one difference in the world, what would it be?*

Notice how the questions invite one answer. The more answers your prospects give, they more likely it is the one thing that counts will be lost in the waffle. One interesting answer tells you exactly what fires your prospect and gives you an entry point into the business.

You'll also notice the questions are very similar to the ones I asked you at the beginning of the book. That's because they work.

TIP #4: Go After Successful People

Your success will depend on how successful the people you sponsor become, so look for the most talented people you can find. Don't shy away from approaching successful people.

In the past few years I have noticed a significant increase in the number of professionals entering direct selling, sometimes from necessity but increasingly from choice. Young people especially value freedom and flexibility over certainty, and opportunity over security. Frequent career changes are the norm for the current generation of business entrepreneurs.

High performers have a confidence that comes from understanding that winning attitudes transfer from one profession to another, and that if you're ambitious, talented, and hard-working, you're going to succeed at anything you do, including building a successful direct selling organization.

When you meet a corporate professional, I suggest an approach along these lines:

With your successful track record I imagine you can choose any job you want. May I ask you a question? With all the skills and experiences you have, why are you working for someone else? Why aren't you starting your own business?

TIP #5: Don't Spill All the Beans

Let curiosity drive your prospect to the next step. Your first approach should raise interest so your prospect will meet with you. If you explain everything at the first contact, you take away the motivation and reason to meet again. Worse, you risk a response based on impulse. When we're undecided, the easiest route is to decline.

The more your prospects get to know you and like you, the more likely it is they will join, so always have a next step in place, whether it's a phone call, chat over coffee, or invitation to an event. If you're not organized at the start of the race, how can you possibly hope to support a new recruit to the finish line?

You will lessen the chance of your prospect canceling an appointment if you confirm appointments the day before, and increase sign-ups if you follow up within forty-eight hours, while the fire is still smoldering.

TIP #6: Make It Easy for Prospects to Join

Explaining that all direct sellers are independent contractors who choose when they work and how often they work will attract more interest than implying a bigger commitment is expected.

For example, one huge advantage of direct selling is that you can start a business while still working a full-time job. Make sure you talk about the wide variety of reasons why it pays to blend a small business with a full-time job:

* ★ An alternative to working overtime
* ★ The tax breaks that come with running a business from home (my favorite)

- ★ Extra income security in a shrinking job market
- ★ A stop-gap career between jobs
- ★ An opportunity to test the waters without diving into the deep end
- ★ A new career without the expense of retraining
- ★ Diversion from a job that lacks satisfaction
- ★ A fun vacation job (perfect for teachers)
- ★ A free trip to aim for and achieve each year (fully paid vacation)

Don't forget the person who decides to quit her job to stay home with the kids. Thousands of moms grapple with the life-changing experience of becoming a full-time stay-at-home mom. Direct selling can give them a chance to be the mom their kids deserve and to earn much-needed income at the same time.

When two incomes morph into one, most households have cash-flow problems to deal with. However, doing one party a week will most likely appeal more to a new mom than will doing three. By setting the expectation bar lower, you raise the number of people who will rise to the challenge. Most successful direct sellers started with small, short-term goals that expanded when they had a taste of success.

Your customers will always be your best prospects. Service them regularly to strengthen your relationships and look for clues as to when and how to get them to take the next step into the business.

There are many ways to stay in touch with your customers and keep them satisfied:

- ★ Offer every new customer two ways to order by saying, *You can order direct from me or you can sign up to order your products wholesale, as I do. Which do you prefer?*
- ★ The second order is always the hardest to get. Thank every new customer with a gift card for 10 percent off the next purchase. Add a thirty-day expiration date so you have

a reason to call back and say, *I wanted to make sure you didn't miss out on the 10 percent gift card I gave you.*

★ Give each customer a loyalty card with the second order entitling her to free products after a certain number (or dollar value) of purchases.

★ Don't neglect customers who sign up as wholesale buyers. The more contact you have, the stronger your relationship will be and the greater your chance of encouraging them to become active Distributors.

★ Make it easy to reach your customers by asking for cell phone numbers and e-mail addresses. While it may be difficult to reach people at home, and you should not intrude at work, you'll have no trouble reaching their e-mail or cell phone.

★ Ask satisfied clients for referrals, and give both the referring and referred client a voucher for 10 percent (or a dollar amount) off the next purchase. Rewarding customers for referrals will encourage them to refer business to you. Offering an incentive to the referred client will give you a reason to call that person.

★ Send postcards to announce new products, specials, or promotions. For example: *Stop paying retail for your favorite products. Become a representative and enjoy wholesale prices.* Postcards are easy to produce, are inexpensive to mail, and you can guarantee they'll be read, unlike letters, which may not be opened.

★ Send out customer e-newsletters—short, interesting, and informative. Give value. It won't work if it's solely a sales flyer. Share tips, news, and usage suggestions. Highlight a maximum of two products in each newsletter, and always add an incentive to book, buy, or join. A catchy heading will increase your chances of customers opening it. Newsy, short communications will increase your chances of their reading it.

★ Make them feel special. Hold customer appreciation nights, invite customers to product previews, and create special offers that can be redeemed at your open home events.

★ Show your appreciation. Send your customers an annual holiday card thanking them for their business and offering an irresistible January special. It's a great way to end the year and start the next year strong.

The bottom line is that if you're not communicating with your customers, you can be sure someone else is. Keeping in touch is critical to building and maintaining relationships.

TIP #7: Identify the Best Prospects in Advance

The more doors you open into your business, the more people will come in. By identifying your most likely prospects before you start your presentation, you'll be able to target them especially.

Sponsoring is about matchmaking. It's finding people who are perfect for your business because your business is perfect for them. When you know who is most likely to be interested, you'll know exactly who to target, and how.

Based on the hundreds of thousands of direct sellers I meet, I can tell you that certain people are more likely to start a business, based on their background, skills, experiences, education, work history, circumstances, and ambitions. In fact, 90 percent of them will belong to one or more of these ten groups:

★ Hostesses
★ Guests at parties
★ Existing customers
★ Teachers
★ Artistic, creative people
★ Nurses
★ Engineers
★ Former cheerleaders

★ Former direct sellers
★ Moms (90 percent of all direct sellers are women)

My book *Be a Recruiting Superstar* is the result of my research into why people become direct sellers and what they did before they became direct sellers. It's a guide to identifying your most likely prospects so you can create a prospect-shopping list. It tells you why people are likely to join, and what to say to ensure they do. Always think:

Who will be interested in my business?
Why will they be interested?

No matter whom it is you're approaching, make sure you can always say, *I'm talking to you because* . . . Here's how to finish that sentence with different prospects:

Someone you look up to . . . *I really admire you.*
A customer who looks great . . . *you always look amazing. I wish I could take you to all my parties as a model.*
Someone who has benefited from using the skincare . . . *your experiences would help others. Many people don't know where to start when it comes to choosing the best skincare products.*
A customer who is always friendly . . . *I always feel good when I call you. You're one of my favorite customers and I would love to work with you.*
A host . . . *your party was so successful and you have such amazing friends. I think you'd be a natural.*
A close friend or sibling . . . *I thought of how much fun it would be for us to work together.*

If you're unsure about approaching friends or family, you may think differently after this story. I was presenting workshops during an incentive cruise on the days the ship was at sea. When one of the achievers introduced me to her top consultant she said, "This is my sister Lisa. I recruited her a year ago and we're sharing a cabin. The best thing about working together is we have never been as close as we are now."

You cannot control other people's decisions, but you can control how many people you reach out to and how well you present your business.

TIP #8: Make Them an Offer They Can't Refuse

Few prospects realize that the value they get from the company they choose to partner with far exceeds their investment. That alone separates direct selling from any other business, where you have to put up all the cost and take all the risk. I'm certain more people would join if they fully appreciated the value of the opportunity they have been given.

This is a powerful way to explain the incredible value and opportunity that comes in the starter kit:

> Let's talk about how much it costs to get started. I'm not sure of the exact amount but it would be a few thousand dollars. But here is the good news. You don't pay that. All you pay is $ . . . toward your starter kit and that includes over $ . . . worth of products, and enough supplies for your first month.
>
> The company basically sponsors you into the business, and you get the most amazing training and support from day one. That means you risk nothing to start and you'll lose nothing if you decide it's not for you (although I doubt that will happen, as we have too much fun). But you can even keep the products.

By discussing the value of the kit you highlight the incredible opportunity you have to offer.

TIP #9: Genuine Compliments Create Good Will

The best way to make your prospects feel good about your business is to make them feel good about themselves. Use phrases such as:

> *I would love to work with you.*
> *You're exactly who we are looking for.*
> *We're a fun group and you would definitely fit in.*
> *You would be such a pleasure to work with. You're always so upbeat and cheerful.*
> *Did you know you're one of my best customers? You would make a great consultant.*
> *Your party was my best this month and I'd love to have you on my team.*

When you're generous with genuine compliments, you'll find that even if your prospects decline they'll feel flattered that you approached them, especially if you take the stress out of the approach by saying, *This business isn't for everyone. I would love to work with you, but if I tell you a little more, you'll know if it's for you.*

When you hear an objection, don't argue with it. Agree with it. If your prospect says, *I just don't see myself as a salesperson* and you respond, *You'd be great*, you're ignoring a genuine concern.

Agreeing with the objection shows you care about your prospect's concerns. When your prospect says, *I just don't see myself as a salesperson*, you say, *I agree. You don't come across that way at all. Do you want to know why I approached you? It's because you come across as genuine, and people respond to that more than a pushy sales pitch.*

If you give your prospects genuine compliments and respond to their concerns, no matter what happens, you've shown professionalism. You can be sure that the next time you call they'll be happy to hear from you.

TIP #10: Never Fear Rejection

Rejection is part of the process of sifting through your prospects to find the positive, enthusiastic ones who will recognize the amazing opportunity you're offering them. You have to work the numbers. Picture this scenario: Your first prospect is too busy. Your second isn't interested. Your third says yes and then at the last minute changes her mind. If you stop at three it's over. You have to move on to number four. Buoy your spirits by reminding yourself that you could be just one approach away from your next recruit.

Don't let the fear of rejection sabotage your business. Identify your fear factor and address it. For most of us it's not the asking, and it's not the "No." It's what to say after the "No." And that's why so many direct sellers say something that's sure to scare off a prospect forever, such as *I'll be here if you ever change your mind.* Ouch!

I created this simple technique to help me exit the situation without losing my customer, friend, or host: When someone says "No," I smile and say, "I'm sure you get asked all the time."

It's a warm compliment that leaves my prospect feeling good, and my confidence intact.

Never forget there's only one guaranteed way you can fail to sponsor, and that is to not ask.

CHAPTER SEVEN

Walk the Talk

Your team will do as you do, not as you say.
—MARY CHRISTENSEN

Your direct selling business gives you many privileges, not the least of them being mastery over your income, your life, and your destiny. It also gives you responsibilities. Being the role model your Distributors deserve is one of them.

Every person in your organization will join with different experiences, circumstances, talents, and priorities. What they'll have in common is this: They deserve a leader who walks the talk. As a direct selling leader you're champion, cheerleader, and coach of a volunteer organization. While corporate CEOs can lead by dominance, you must lead by influence.

★ Influential leaders inspire others to become the best they can be.
★ Influential leaders exude confidence in the business. They know that the stronger they are, the weaker the doubts of their team members will be.
★ Influential leaders are role models who lead from the front. They know their Distributors are independent operators and they cannot tell them what to do.

They can only control the example they set for the Distributors.

★ Influential leaders live the promise that direct selling allows ordinary people to live extraordinary lives. The message they send is, *If I can do it, you can do it.* Even if the leaders possess exceptional talents, they understand that strengths can be liabilities if they convey the impression that only gifted people can succeed.

★ Influential leaders know that everything they do will filter through their organization. They ask this question every day: *If everyone in my organization does what I'm doing, what kind of business will I have?*

★ Above all, influential leaders are pragmatists who understand that the greatest act of leadership is to be a glowing example that the business works if you do.

Concentrating your time, energy, and resources on the most productive activities will have a compounding effect on your business. Your team members will do what you do. If you're not doing enough, or you're doing the wrong things, your mistakes will be duplicated many times over as your Distributors mimic them. You can't do one thing and expect your team to do another.

If your organization is growing, congratulations. What you've been doing has successfully brought you to this point. Don't change now. Many promoting leaders become so entranced with their new status that they change the way they allocate their time. This is a huge error of judgment. To ensure continuing growth, do more of what you already have been doing.

If your business is stagnant, change what you're doing. Evaluate the skills and work habits you have, and where you're lacking. While it makes sense to build on your strengths, it's equally important to eliminate your weaknesses. Even the biggest structure can be toppled by the smallest fault.

If you're a new or aspiring leader, don't wait until you have the title to assume the mantle of leadership. Set the standard you want your future team to follow by thinking and acting as though you're already heading a large organization.

Start by making sure you're fully engaged in your business. The more hours you invest, the faster you'll advance. Not administrative hours or planning hours, but on-the-job hours, spent networking, making presentations, meeting face-to-face, working the phones, and being active in social media.

Thinking about what you're going to do doesn't count. One small step will take you farther than one hundred grand intentions.

Focus on the most important tasks first. As we all know, they are not always the most appealing. Success comes to those who aren't afraid to tackle the tough tasks. It comes to those who work both when they feel like it and when they don't.

The question should never be, *Will this business work?* but rather, *Will I work?* Activity will drive your income. Most of us have to juggle work, family, and business commitments, and that requires setting priorities and developing discipline. You're not going to have enough time to do the things you want to do, so don't waste time doing things you don't need to do. Focus plus discipline equals results.

Every promoting leader should spend half of all available time on personal activity. I wanted to be the parent my kids deserved, and I wanted to support them financially. Once I set my priorities I found it easy to allocate my time and even easier to let go of anything that didn't fit into my plan. When you know what you want, you know what to do.

TAKE THESE STEPS TO LEAD YOUR TEAM BY EXAMPLE

Step One
Work a separate calendar for your business.   I recommend one that displays one month per page. Jumbling your personal and business appointments together can conceal your true situation.

With a separate calendar you'll always know exactly how many appointments you've scheduled without having to sift through your personal, family, and social commitments.

Step Two

List the sales and sponsoring targets that will help you attain your goals. If you're aiming for thirty new Distributors, list the numbers 1 to 30 on a separate page in your calendar and add the name of each new Distributor before the ink dries on the agreement form. The growing list of names will keep you motivated.

If you're aiming for a promotion or incentive, break it down to weekly targets and keep track in your calendar. You'll know at a glance if you need to pick up the pace.

Step Three

Commit to working regular hours. Good habits become ingrained through repetition, and every great leader is consistent and persistent. If you share your goals and your rewards with your family they'll be supportive.

A regular schedule of two parties or presentations a week with an average of ten guests attending will yield a thousand new contacts a year. Industry averages indicate that one in every five hosts becomes a Distributor, so that almost guarantees you twenty new recruits.

If you commit to making ten business-generating calls a day, don't stop until you've made them. Making ten calls (about one hour of phone time) each weekday for fifty weeks adds up to 2,500 calls a year.

My greatest challenge was making calls, so I devised a simple trick that worked for me. I placed ten bangles on my left wrist every morning as a promise I would make ten calls. Every time I made a call I transferred one bangle to my right wrist. It focused me on making calls instead of worrying about rejection, and it transformed my business. Picture the impact you could make on your business if everyone in your organization made ten calls each day.

You work hard to gain your customers. Take care of them. Inconsistent servicing is the number one reason customers drift away. Your income is based on sales, so your customers are your greatest assets. Servicing your customers is a golden opportunity to make money and build relationships at the same time.

If you need a trick to help you make the calls, try placing ten order forms next to your landline or on your countertop each morning. Every time you pass them make a servicing call:

> *I'm just about to place an order and your favorite bread mix is on special this week. Would you like me to add a couple of bags to my order for you?*
>
> *We've just released a new energy bar and I'm giving a free sample to every customer who places an order this week. I only have twenty to give away and I wanted to make sure you didn't miss out. You've probably almost finished your protein shake. Shall I order another box for you?*
>
> *Has your family escaped the latest flu that's going round? So far we've been lucky but practically all my son's classmates have been sick. I'm giving all my family an extra supplement every morning until it passes and I thought you might want to do the same. Do you want me to add some onto my order today for you?*
>
> *The company has just added three new charms to our signature bracelet collection. One of them has 'you' written all over it. I'll e-mail you a picture and call back this afternoon to see if you love it as much as I think you will. They're not going to be a regular item. We have them only while supplies last.*
>
> *Great news! The company has just announced that some of our best-selling fragrance bars are on a two-for-one offer for the month. We expect them to sell out, so I'm calling all my customers to make sure you don't miss out. Are you*

interested? It may pay to order two sets, as we don't usually have our top sellers on such a great special. I'm stocking up, as they make great gifts.

Step Four

Project success. You're marketing financial freedom. If you look like a happy, successful person, you'll find it easier to attract your A-team.

Body language sends the most powerful message of all. Demonstrate your confidence with great posture, a winning smile, and ready eye contact.

Dress to impress. You don't need to spend a fortune to stay abreast of current trends, and outdated or ill-fitting clothes will contradict your message of success. Whether you opt for smart casual or business attire, make sure your grooming is immaculate.

Step Five

Communicate a clear, consistent message. If you cannot articulate exactly what you represent, what chance do you have of inspiring others to share your vision?

Communication is a two-way process. It's not enough to be a persuasive speaker. You must be a good listener. Give people your full attention and don't allow yourself to be distracted by what's happening around you. These small actions will lead to big results:

★ Turn off your cell phone when you have company.
★ Show a genuine interest in others.
★ Don't be an interrupter. Formulating a response in your head when the other person is speaking is as bad as an interjection. Both show that you're neither interested nor engaged.
★ Look at the people you're addressing and change tack if you read clues such as folded arms, loss of eye

contact, and restlessness. All of these show you're not connecting.
* Invite and welcome feedback and questions.
* Develop curiosity.

Step Six

Consistently walk the talk.   Leaders demonstrate belief in their products by becoming their own best customers. They turn their homes into competitor-free zones. Your products are your calling card. The more you embrace them, the more credibility you'll have.

* If your business is beauty, does your skin glow with vitality?
* If you represent clothing and accessories, do the designs you wear complement your body shape? Do your accessories attract compliments?
* If your products promise weight loss, do you have impressive before-and-after photos to show? If you're a work in progress, do you have an inspiring story to share?
* If you sell candles, do you brighten your own home with candlelight every night?
* If you represent cooking and entertaining products, do you share recipes and host themed parties for friends and family?

Leaders demonstrate belief in their business by sharing it every chance they get. They carry sponsoring literature, agreements, product catalogs, samples, incentive brochures, and business cards with them at all times. Scrambling through your purse for a business card or producing a dog-eared brochure from the trunk of your car are the marks of an amateur.

Leaders demonstrate belief in their corporate partners by embracing their companies' programs and events wholeheartedly. They are first to commit to an event and believe leadership is a commitment that includes showing up at the national convention and leadership conference.

Leaders are visible—not only when they're on center stage but also when others take their turn in the spotlight. They sit in the front row at events to show support for the speakers. They applaud achievers who are team members as well as those who are not. Elite leaders never retreat to the hallway when others are presenting or being applauded.

Aiming for every incentive your company offers makes you living proof that the rewards of success are attainable. Leaders are excited when an incentive trip is announced and they commit to achieving it. They're first to say, *I'm going. Who's coming with me?*

Leaders demonstrate belief in the profession by building networks of professionals who share their passion. They seek out and support other direct sellers who represent noncompeting products. By projecting a clear, consistent message on all fronts you give your team members a standard to aim for. If you send conflicting messages, they'll be conflicted.

The bottom line is this: The better you are, the better your Distributors will be, and the better your Distributors are, the more successful your business will be. As goes the leader, so goes the team. The pace of the leader always determines the pace of the pack.

PART TWO

Team Leadership

*Your greatest reward as a leader will be
to know that you're the catalyst for others'
successes.*

—Mary Christensen

CHAPTER EIGHT

Find Their Fire

*You'll get what you want by helping others
get what they want.*
—MARY CHRISTENSEN

Roll out the red carpet for every new recruit. New recruits are the life breath of your business, and they come to you brimming with potential. Your challenge is to turn that promise into performance.

Here are some sobering statistics from the Direct Selling Association: Half of all direct sellers exit the business in the first three months, and four out of five leave within the first year.

Some of the reasons for the high dropout rate are beyond your control, but inexperienced, indifferent, or misguided leadership are key contributors. Be the exception and you'll reap the rewards.

THE WELCOME INTERVIEW

The relationship you establish with your new recruits at the start will set the scene for the relationship you'll have with them going forward.

As soon as the agreement is signed, set up a one-on-one Welcome interview with every new recruit. This is the official start of your business relationship, so don't skip this step even if a new recruit is someone you know well.

The purpose of a Welcome interview is twofold:

- ★ To learn as much as you can about your new recruit's lifestyle, circumstances, and expectations, so you can offer the most appropriate support
- ★ To find the goal that will power the recruit's first year in the business

What better way can there be to start your Welcome interview than this?

Congratulations on starting your new business. I'm so excited you've chosen to join us, and I'm looking forward to working with you. I expect we'll be spending a lot of time together, and today is about getting to know each other and finding out what you want from your business.

A Welcome interview should be a conversation, not an interrogation, but the more questions you ask the clearer picture you'll have of your recruit's expectations and circumstances:

- ★ *How long have you lived here?*
- ★ *Do you own or rent your home?*
- ★ *Where did you live before you moved here?*
- ★ *Are you married or single?*
- ★ *How long have you been together?*
- ★ *When is your next anniversary?*
- ★ *How many children do you have?*
- ★ *What are their names?*
- ★ *How old are they?*
- ★ *Do you have other family members living close by?*
- ★ *What does your family most like to do together?*

★ *What else do you do for fun?*
★ *What do you do to relax?*
★ *When's your birthday?*
★ *Do you have another job?*
★ *Is it full-time or part-time?*
★ *Have you always had that job?*
★ *What does your partner do for a living?*
★ *Have you ever been in business before?*
★ *Have you ever been in direct selling before?*
★ *Have you been invited before?*
★ *What was different this time?*
★ *What motivated you to start your own business?*
★ *What appealed to you most about our company?*

The answers will yield a ton of valuable information you can use to keep your new recruit fired and inspired. Make sure you take notes for a personal file that you create for each team member. Enter key dates such as birthdays or anniversaries into a file that you use to track team achievements and milestones so you can send a card or message without having to look up the details every time.

FIND THEIR GOAL

Now it's time to establish the new recruit's goal. Each business must begin the way yours did, with a goal the recruit is passionate about.

Avoid the rookie leader's mistake of rushing into training. There will be plenty of time to teach the skills and tools. An exciting goal will keep your new recruit energized through the first year and keep her from quitting when she hits the inevitable roadblocks.

Helping your recruit to establish her goal will be an enjoyable experience for both of you, and will strengthen the bonds you began to form during the lead-up to the decision to join. Sometimes it will be easy to find the right goal, and other times it will take more time and skill. Don't let impatience be your downfall. The recruit's goal will be the flashing beacon that keeps her excited, focused, and on track.

Sharing your own goal is a great way to encourage your new recruit to open up to you. For example:

> *Every year we all set a goal to work toward. It's one of the fun parts of the business. Last year was our tenth wedding anniversary and my goal was to take my husband on a romantic getaway to Tahiti. It was even better than we imagined, but this year I have a more practical goal.*
>
> *This year my goal is to build a six-month emergency fund. My husband's job isn't as secure as we once thought it was, and we'll both be happier if we know we can pay the bills while he looks for another job.*
>
> *I'm excited to know what your goal is. If you could achieve one thing from your business this year, what would it be?*

Remember, it's the gap between what we have and what we want that drives us. A goal comes from the gap between where we are in our lives and where we want to be.

Your new recruits will all have different gaps, and the way to reveal them is to ask questions. The more skilled you are at asking questions, the sooner you'll find goals with enough firepower to drive the recruits through their most vulnerable year in business.

Even if you've already asked questions during the sponsoring interview, ask them again. Circumstances can change. A new recruit will almost certainly have a different perspective once she has signed the agreement.

The questions have to be interesting so your new recruit will enjoy opening up to you. They have to be focused, so you can find the one goal special enough to ensure that the recruit stays motivated during the learning process.

The questions must also be appropriate for the situation.

There's no point talking about luxury cruises if your new recruit needs cash to put gas in the car or pay off a pressing debt.

A young, single person will have aspirations and expectations that are different from those of someone who is married and mortgaged. Younger recruits are more likely to be interested in a quick payoff for their efforts. Adapt your questions to suit.

You'll find this process easier if you've paid attention to what recruits have been saying to you during the lead-up to signing. It may be helpful to review the seven steps to finding the right goal (see Chapter 1). In addition, you can use the following questions as a guide:

★ *What difference would an extra $200 a week make to your life?*
★ *What would you do with it?*
★ *How different would your life be if you earned $1,000 a week?*
★ *How do you feel about credit card debt?*
★ *Do you love to travel?*
★ *Can you describe your dream vacation?*
★ *If you had $10,000 in the bank today, how would you spend it?*

Give your recruits time to think about their answers. If you start prompting, you'll most likely hear the first thought that comes to mind or the answer they think you want to hear. If you take your time you'll gather a goldmine of priceless information.

Only intervene if someone answers *I don't know,* or *I can't think of one right now.*

Goals are very personal, and some people may be reluctant to open up about their true goals. That is when your skill as an empathetic, interested listener will come into play.

This entire profession is driven by goals, and if you don't establish an exciting goal at the start you'll be pushing uphill to keep your new team members motivated. Exciting goals will keep them energized and prevent them from becoming discouraged or defeated when things don't work out as planned.

Setting a small or short-term goal is fine at the start as long as it has punch. Many top achievers start with small goals that expand as they start to see the potential of the business. Unrealistic expectations can actually be counterproductive. The fastest route out of this business is disappointment.

If a new recruit is raring to go, it's fine to set an ambitious goal as long as you both agree that it's attainable and that the recruit is willing to invest the time to achieve it. A goal without a time commitment is a pipe dream. Realistic expectations are even more critical. The more ambitious the goal, the more time and commitment will be needed.

If your new recruits have difficulty narrowing their goals to just one, gently remind them that they'll be juggling their business and personal responsibilities, and encourage them to focus on only one goal at a time.

Share my golden rule of goal setting: *One goal, one year, one step at a time.*

Once a recruit's goal has been established, encourage her to display it on her screensaver, calendar cover, or goal board. Suggest looking at the goal at least once a day to stay motivated.

One of the greatest threats to your new recruits' success is how little it costs to start a direct selling business. Because they have invested so little, it's easy to underestimate the potential of the business. When they hit their first speed bump, they can walk away having risked nothing and lost nothing. Easy in, easy out.

That's why you should gain each recruit's commitment to achieving her goal by saying:

> *I think it's a fantastic goal and I'm excited for you. I can't wait to see you achieving it and I'm sure you can't wait to get started.*

I promise to give you the support you need. All I ask from you is to promise me two things.

The first is that you won't underestimate the potential of your new business just because it costs so little to start. Your starter kit is an investment the company has made in you. If you're willing to work and you're willing to learn, nothing can stop you from achieving your goal.

The second is that you won't give up until you achieve what you've set out to achieve. I know you can do it. If you hit a few speed bumps, as most of us do when we're learning, I'll help you get back on track. But your goal is worth working for, and I want to know that you're as committed to it as I am to helping you.

What is so great about this business is that you cannot fail if you do not quit before you succeed.

Keep a record of every team member's goals so you can keep them excited about achieving them. When they hit a rough patch you can say:

It can be frustrating when things don't go according to plan, and I feel for you. But I see you (driving that new car . . .) and I'll help you work through this. So, instead of feeling discouraged, think of what you have to gain. I know you can do it.

Small goals are the stepping-stones to larger goals. Almost all direct selling companies have a Fast Start Rewards program that offers new recruits an opportunity to earn bonus rewards in their first three to four months.

The companies do this because they know the first few months are the hardest, so don't take the Fast Start program for granted. It's a step-by-step guide to what needs to be done during the first months. Get every new recruit excited about the bonus rewards by saying:

Now that we have established your key goal, I have some great news for you. One of the ways the company supports you at the start is by giving you the opportunity to earn bonus rewards in your first months. It's an incredible opportunity to (build your kit, earn extra cash . . .)

Make sure your recruits understand that the rewards are available one time only and that they have deadlines. Stress the urgency of the Fast Start Rewards so they'll start working toward them immediately.

Most Fast Start Rewards programs have a sponsoring component that will help focus your new recruit on sponsoring from the start. Everyone knows someone who could be a possible recruit, and if you wait too long to identify that person the opportunity may never come again. Think about it. If every new person recruits just one other person, you will already have replaced any recruit who may subsequently leave.

There are many ways you can identify that possible new recruit. One is to invite your own recruit to bring someone to training. Try saying this:

You're going to have a great time at training, so why don't you bring someone with you? Of everyone you know, who do you think is most likely to be interested in doing what you're doing?

Give your recruit time to mentally scroll through her contacts. Follow up any leads immediately so they can start together. When two people join together, they both do better.

Another way to identify the person is to introduce the next incentive trip and then ask this question:

How excited are you about earning a fully paid vacation?

Most likely the recruit will say, *Very excited.*

That leads into your saying, *Let's imagine you've earned the trip and you can take one person with you. Not your partner or children, but a friend, family member, or work colleague. Who would be your perfect traveling companion? Who would you choose?*

When the recruit names someone, ask, *Why don't you call her, tell her how excited you are about your new business and ask if she's interested in doing it too? You can work on achieving the trip together.*

Conclude the Welcome interview by outlining your new recruit's next steps, including the first training, which should be scheduled the same week as the Welcome interview so the recruit won't lose momentum.

A fun, positive way to end the Welcome interview is to take a photo of your new recruit, ready to use when you share her achievements and milestones in your team newsletter or on your team Facebook page.

CHAPTER NINE

Create a Realistic Roadmap

The fastest route out of the business is disappointment.
—MARY CHRISTENSEN

A few years ago I participated in a Leadership Retreat where business sessions were alternated with outdoor challenges. All of the activities were designed to test our courage and stretch our comfort zones.

The first day I was blindfolded and driven deep into a forest. When the blindfold was removed I was given water, a compass, and a whistle for emergencies, and challenged to find my way out of the forest. To heighten the challenge, I had to follow a strict southeast route. No detours or deviations were allowed, which meant at one point I had to swim fully clothed across a river. But with my feet (mostly) on the ground I completed the challenge with minimum drama.

The next challenge was to rappel a steep cliff. Jumping backward into a chasm hundreds of feet below required only one act of courage: the leap. Once I was airborne there was no choice but to keep going, so I successfully accomplished that task as well.

Later that night, when the challenge for the next day was announced, the doubts started to creep in. It was rock climbing.

I spent a restless night fretting about the challenge. By morning I had convinced myself rock climbing was beyond the farthest limits of my comfort zone. I decided to accompany the group to the rock but make a last-minute excuse to avoid the climb.

We disembarked into a forest clearing a few yards from the rock for a briefing. One of the rules of the day was that only one person at a time could approach the rock. The rest of us had to wait in the clearing, where trees obscured any view of the rock. That meant none of us could watch the others make their ascent.

When it was my turn a surprise awaited me. It was less than half as high as I had pictured and had deep grooves for hand- and footholds. I realized I could do it, so I shelved my opt-out plan and stepped up to attempt the climb. The instructors helped me gain my first foothold, and then I was on my own. Inch by inch I climbed my way to the top. As I pulled myself over the rim my mind was already celebrating another challenge accomplished. Yes!

My celebrations were premature. I was not at the top of the rock. Another rock face, set a few feet back and invisible from the ground, loomed in front of me. Now I understood why we had to approach the rock one person at a time. The climb was in two parts.

On the second stage the footholds were shallower and the spaces between them bigger. I had accomplished half the challenge, however, so I decided to keep moving. This time it took longer. My arm and leg muscles ached and my fingernails were soon filed away by the gritty rock. But buoyed by success and the cheers of the "support crew" below me, I hauled myself to the top.

Triumph. I had made it. Except . . . you guessed it. Another ledge, another rock face. Now that I had made it this far, defeat seemed unthinkable. Fueled by a potent mix of success, adrenaline, and *I'll show them* determination, I pressed upward.

Soon my heart was pounding and my fingertips were raw from the friction of bare skin against stone. It took every ounce of will to keep going, but I was assured it was the last stage of the climb. You can imagine the thrill of accomplishment when I finally reached the top.

The personal lesson I learned that day is that I had wasted a lot of time and energy worrying about a challenge I was clearly capable of accomplishing.

The leadership lessons I learned were even more profound:

- ★ The instructors knew I could do it. They gave me the opportunity to find out I could do it.
- ★ Instead of presenting me with an overwhelming challenge, they divided the climb into manageable stages.
- ★ Because they helped me onto the rock, I was on my way before I had time to overthink the challenge ahead of me.
- ★ The small success I tasted at the start was enough to keep me motivated through the more difficult stages.
- ★ At every stage of the climb I was encouraged and applauded.

There's a close parallel between my experience and what all recruits experience as they start their businesses. Most start out feeling excited but also a little apprehensive about the challenge ahead of them. That's why you must set them up for success in the first critical months. Be generous with your time and support, as many of them have not have been in business before and must acquire the necessary skills and attitudes from scratch.

When you factor in the time and energy it takes to sign them, the time you invest helping your new recruits navigate their first ninety days makes good business sense.

Prepare and equip them to start strong and stay the distance by creating a realistic roadmap for all new recruits. A series of small successes will act as the stepping-stones to larger success.

THE FIRST THIRTY DAYS

Their first thirty days will be a honeymoon period. Their enthusiasm will be at a peak and they'll have plenty of contacts to approach. But starting a new business can be overwhelming. Rather than overload your recruits with information, focus on the key steps they need to take to start earning. Think:

What do they need to know now?
What do they need to do now?

★ If your company offers a Fast Start Rewards program, make it the blueprint for their first three months. Make each step as clear as possible by preparing a simple "cheat sheet" that lists deadlines for the Fast Start Rewards, alongside dates and topics for training.

★ Make sure they understand that the more hours they work, the more rewards they'll earn. Create urgency by stressing that the Fast Start Rewards are a one-time-only opportunity. Success is a powerful motivator.

★ Encourage them to work separate calendars for their businesses and to allocate specific times to work. Suggest they block those times in their calendars as a constant reminder of the commitment they have made. Make sure they commit to participating in team meetings, conference calls, and the national conference by entering the dates in their calendars immediately.

★ Stress the importance of using the products themselves. Product fact sheets and third-party endorsements are no substitute for personal experiences.

★ The longer their contacts lists are, the sooner they'll master the art of making calls. Challenge them to keep adding to their lists and suggest they note cell phone numbers and e-mail addresses alongside names at the start. Otherwise they'll be searching for contact details when they should be making calls.

★ Without bookings they don't have a business, so making calls has to be their top priority. Set an expectation of ten calls a day. You'll lessen the impact of rejection if you explain that hearing "No" is normal. If they have realistic expectations, they'll be less likely to be discouraged by a run of "No thanks" responses.

★ Keep heavy-duty training to a minimum. No one is going to be motivated by the policies and procedures manual, or detailed explanations of the compensation plan. Focus instead on the core skills of booking, selling, and sponsoring, and how to integrate all three into every one-on-one or group presentation. If your corporate manual is a blockbuster, point them to key areas they can read first.

★ Invite them to accompany you to one of your appointments or parties within two weeks so they can observe firsthand how to conduct a successful presentation.

★ Encourage all of your recruits to hold a Launch Party as soon as possible, so their friends, family, and associates can celebrate with them and experience the products themselves.

★ Attend each recruit's Launch Party to show your support and help all of them secure their first bookings. Rather than play a key role, focus on mixing and mingling with the guests so you can get to know each recruit's inner circle. The Launch Party is a celebration, and a soft-sell approach will work better than a heavy-handed one.

★ When the time is right, ask to say a few words:

Thanks everyone for joining us to celebrate the start of Paige's new business. We are thrilled she has chosen our company and we know she is going to be a huge success.

We couldn't think of a better way to start her business than celebrating with the people she cares about, and I'm sure Paige appreciates your support.

You may be wondering what you can do to help her. Because she is learning, what she needs most right now is help with her first bookings. Hosting a party will help her immensely, and that's why you'll receive some exciting rewards for doing so.

★ Outline the host rewards and hand out party bags with a small thank-you gift and hosting information inside so your new recruit can follow up the leads you helped create.

THE FIRST SIXTY DAYS

At some stage during the first sixty days, reality will start to set in. Most new recruits achieve their initial results from sales to close friends and family. If they have mined their inner circle of contacts without reaching out to a wider range of contacts, the second month will be harder. Generating bookings from their initial presentations is a top priority for all new recruits and needs special emphasis in your training. Stress the importance of using every party or presentation as a stepping-stone to new bookings. The number one reason recruits leave the business is because they run out of leads.

Recruits who didn't achieve their first month target may be already starting to doubt the business, or even themselves. Suggest they draw a line over the first month and keep facing forward. There's no point looking in the rearview mirror when the opportunity is in front of them.

Monitor their progress closely, always watching for flags. Green flags are consistent sales and future bookings. A Rising Star is emerging.

Red flags are low sales or a sparse schedule of forward bookings. They forecast danger if you don't act fast. Keep your recruits focusing forward, but work closely with those who are struggling in order to identify the problem. The sooner they fix small problems, the less likely it is they'll balloon into big problems.

If the recruits' complaints center on *No one is interested/has the money/the time*, they need help with making calls. Their enthusiasm may be coming across as a sales pitch, or they're not taking the time to connect with their prospects. I recommend role-playing a few calls to pinpoint the problem.

If they started strong but they're not generating forward bookings, they need help expanding their contacts. This is the hardest part of the business for many new recruits, but no one can build a business on friends and family alone. The sooner they learn to generate forward bookings, the more stable their business will become.

Taking an empathetic approach to their concerns—for example, *Most of us hit a period when we need to work harder at moving beyond our comfort* zone—will help make this less stressful as you coach them to book consistently.

Whatever their first sixty-day results are, don't let discouragement seep in. Some recruits will take longer to find their feet than others. Applaud their achievements and keep them focusing forward.

THE FIRST NINETY DAYS

Crunch time often comes in the third month. Your strongest recruits will be seeing real results, your steady performers will be settling in, and your lowest performers will be floundering. Some may already be considering leaving the business. Attrition is normal, but how you coach those who are struggling through this critical period could be the deciding factor in whether they knuckle down or drift away.

After ninety days you'll have a clear picture of the direction in which your new recruits are heading. Some will be ready to join your regular training program. Some will have demonstrated the desire, drive, and discipline to move straight into your leadership development program. We'll cover both groups in upcoming chapters.

Whatever their next step will be, you'll have the satisfaction of knowing you gave every new recruit the best possible chance of succeeding.

The overlying lesson is that you cannot start new people in cruise control and expect them to soar. The average dropout rate in the first three months is 50 percent. If your team's performance matches that, you have wasted a huge amount of the time and effort you spent introducing new people to the business.

If you set up your new people for success, monitor their results, and support them through the first three months, they'll start stronger, perform better, and stay longer.

CHAPTER TEN

Build Belief

Treat every newcomer as a Superstar in the making.
—Mary Christensen

The motivation to have more, do more, and be more in our lives comes from within. An influential leader plays a key role in turning desire into performance by building belief into each recruit's business.

When you bolster your people's belief in the products, they'll promote them more enthusiastically. When you bolster their belief in the business, they'll share it more convincingly. When you bolster their belief in themselves, they'll pursue their goals more confidently.

Your experiences have taught you that if you want it, and you're willing to work for it, you can achieve anything you want from your business. Most new recruits have yet to learn that truth, so you'll often find yourself believing in them more than they believe in themselves.

Everyone will rise to his or her true potential. Some will rise higher than others. But you must treat all team members as though they're on a natural progression from Rising Star to Shining Star and ultimately, Superstar. Let their performance indicate when they have reached their peak of brilliance.

As more than 90 percent of direct sellers are women, it is highly likely you'll be leading a predominantly female organization. Women bring many qualities to the profession, but many will overestimate the challenge involved in growing a business and underestimate themselves. We harbor fears and doubts about our abilities that have no basis in reality. Our logical right brain tells us that anything and everything is possible, while our emotional left brain argues that we are somehow unqualified or undeserving. In fact the opposite is true. Women have leadership skills woven into their DNA, and growing a direct selling business will strengthen their talents.

There are many paths to success, and few are as accessible as direct selling. A business degree is the most expensive, a corporate career is the least flexible, and a go-it-alone business is the riskiest. With direct selling, there's little cost and no sacrifice or risk. Your team members will learn as they earn, and grow as their businesses grow. Direct selling is the ultimate personal growth business. If your team members can run a home, raise a family, and organize their lives, they are fully equipped to run a multimillion-dollar business.

When they believe it they'll work harder to achieve it. By helping your team members overcome self-defeating beliefs you open them up to a whole new world of possibilities. Think of a swan and you picture a graceful, elegant bird. How does a swan start out? As an ugly duckling. And yet it is destined to emerge as a beautiful gift of nature.

By signing the agreement your new recruits express the desire to grow. Their goals indicate how they want to grow. What they can gain from you is the steadfast belief that they *will* grow.

Here's what you can say to build belief in a new recruit:

I know you're going to make a huge success of your business and, I suspect, even more than you imagine. I'm sure you're excited and also a little apprehensive about how and where to start. We'll cover all that at training.

But I know you can do it, and I think you know it too. What you'll find is it takes courage and discipline to get your business off to a great start. The confidence will come as you start seeing results.

REINFORCE THEIR BELIEF

Direct selling is an emotional business, and emotions can be fragile. You have to fill and refill your Distributors with belief in their products, their businesses, and themselves, so no matter how many bumps, bruises, and knockdowns they take, there will always be a reservoir of belief to see them through.

Picture filling a bucket with water and carrying it along a bumpy path. It's almost inevitable that some of the water will spill en route. If there are already holes in the bucket, the water will drip away until the bucket is empty. If the bucket is jostled, more will be lost. You have to keep adding more water, just as you have to keep refilling your team members with belief.

Build belief into every layer of your business. When a new catalog is launched, say, *These products are fantastic. I'm already thinking about which of my clients to call first. I'm excited because it's going to help all of us have a huge boost in sales.*

When a new incentive is presented, say, *This is so exciting . . . and achievable. We should all work together to earn it. Let's break it down into weekly targets and commit as a team to achieving it.*

Build belief by sharing positive messages in your training and support programs:

★ *You have what it takes.*
★ *I see huge potential in you.*
★ *If you want it, and you're willing to work for it, you can have it.*
★ *I know you'll be on the trip with us.*

Every time a team member's confidence takes a hit, whether it's from a canceled engagement, a prospect who loses interest at the last minute, or a missed incentive, rebuild that person's shaken confidence before you look for solutions:

That's tough, and I feel for you. But what I admire about you is that you're not a quitter. So, let's move on and look at what you can do to make up for lost ground. Remember, you cannot fail if you do not quit until you succeed.

Influential leaders believe that everyone has the potential to grow beyond their current situation, and some have the potential to grow beyond their wildest imagination. They inspire others to believe that nothing can hold them back except their willingness to fuel negative perceptions, or "stinking thinking."

As Henry Ford said, "*If you think you can do a thing, or you think you can't do a thing, you're right.*"

When we believe it, we set ourselves free to achieve it.

CHAPTER ELEVEN

Be a Strategic Mentor

Give your attention to those who deserve it,
not those who demand it.
—MARY CHRISTENSEN

I t's natural to feel responsible for everyone you sponsor. You want
the best for them, and you know your success will be determined by how successful they become. But every direct seller
signs on as an independent business owner and they are all responsible for their own success.

Time will always be your most precious resource, and the
only way to use it effectively is to spend the bulk of your time
with those who are actively working. Your team members will
have different experiences, expectations, circumstances, and priorities. You have to invest in those who will benefit the most from
your support, and that means new people and those who are producing results.

Just as a bird teaches its young to fly by nudging them out
of the nest, it is never too soon to start steering new Distributors toward independence. That means giving them access to the
training they need, when they need it. This may not always be
when they feel they need it. Growing a business is a steep learning curve, and many direct sellers wrongly assume that the more

training they get, the easier it will be. The only way to learn the job is on the job. More training is not the answer—more experience is the answer.

To express it bluntly, give the bulk of your attention to those who deserve it, not those who demand it. One of the greatest mistakes a leader can make is working with the wrong people. Women are more likely to make that mistake. A disconnect between what we instinctively do as parents and how we run our business is where many leaders go wrong.

Before you start shouldering the responsibility for your team members' success, think of how you raise your children. You know that if you do everything for them they won't learn to survive on their own. You expect them to take responsibility for their actions, and the consequences of their actions.

You reinforce those principles when you teach your children board games. You explain the game and then take turns to move. They make a move, you make a move, and it's their turn again. The only way they'll master the game is to play the game. In the same way, instead of thinking that the more you do for your team members the better chance they will have, take the same *your move, my move, your move* approach to mentoring.

Establishing expectations based on the goals they set for themselves, giving them support and guidance when they need it, and offering honest feedback along the way is the only way to empower your recruits to discover their true potential. To carry them is to cripple them. Being overprotective and accepting promises over performance and excuses over action is a surefire way to stunt their growth.

If you allow your team members to dump their problems on you, you'll teach them to depend on you. By solving their problems for them, you deny them the experiences they need to grow. As you'll learn in the next section, one of the mentors who taught me that lesson was a riding instructor I met in Arizona.

SMALL IN THE SADDLE

Because I have always been a little apprehensive around horses, I decided to build my confidence by gaining some experience at a riding school.

I chose a beginner's trek through a beautiful canyon, and lined up with about twenty other riders to be assigned a mount. When the instructors asked about our riding experience, I volunteered that I was a beginner and they promised me a docile mount. But my "docile" horse immediately sensed my uncertainty. As soon as the instructor's back was turned it headed straight back to the stables. No amount of cajoling could coax him out until the instructor rescued me with a tug on the reins that the horse instantly obeyed.

The first part of the ride was uneventful. Then, as we descended into the canyon, my horse headed for the edge of the path. The trail dropped steeply into the canyon, so my feet were literally hanging over the edge of a precipice. My heart started pumping as I visualized the horse stumbling on the crumbly path and pitching me into the canyon.

When I wasn't worrying about being tossed off the horse, I was worried about catapulting over its head, which it permanently bowed as it foraged for food along the trail.

"Show him who's the boss," the instructor called to me.

"I'm trying," I called back, as I tugged fruitlessly on the reins.

I was relieved when we finally reached a stream that marked the halfway point of our trek. The return journey was all uphill, and I started to relax a little. But there was a snag. The other riders were complaining that the pace was too slow. They wanted more action and pleaded for a chance to gallop, or at least canter back up the trail. I kept silent, confident the instructors wouldn't give way to their demands. But there's no pressure like group pressure, and I was horrified when they agreed to speed things up a little.

They assured us that if any of us wanted to stop, all we had to do was call out and everyone would stop. There was no way I was going to shame myself in public, so I started to canter up the trail. Within seconds I was bumping up and down in the saddle and although I held the reins as tight as I could, I was convinced I was going to fall off. An unpleasant experience was fast turning into a frightening one. Then thankfully someone screamed, "Stop!"

The instructors immediately stopped the horses as the other riders shot thunderous looks at the killjoy—*me*.

I could live with the shame, but it wasn't my day. The instructors had been enjoying the faster pace too, and after a brief discussion they announced that two of them would escort the main group back to the stables while one stayed behind with me. Within seconds, everyone had disappeared up the trail, leaving me with my own instructor. Rather than reassure me it was okay, she said, "You were doing fine. You weren't going to fall off."

When I tried to explain that the pace was too fast, she interrupted and said, "You called stop because you were totally focused on falling."

I started to protest, but my instructor was having none of it. She looked me in the eye and said. "The ones who think about falling off are the only ones who do."

She was right. I'd barely noticed the scenery. I was fixated on falling. But I was embarrassed, so I argued back. "It's not me, the horse is walking too close to the edge."

The instructor wasn't buying my excuses. She shot me a frustrated glance and said, "I'll ride on the outside."

We set off again, and this time I focused on the experience. I began to notice the spectacular scenery. The canyon was alive with birds, and I caught a glimpse of a coyote. We even passed the ruins of an ancient cliff dwelling. It was a wonderful experience, and by the time we reached the stables I was already planning my next ride.

My young instructor was a glowing example of leadership. By challenging my excuses with frankness and honesty, she helped me see that the problem wasn't the horse, or the trail. I was the problem.

Give your recruits space to grow. Being overprotective will deny them an opportunity to discover their strengths, face up to their fears, and move on from their mistakes.

WORK WITH YOUR TOP PERFORMERS

If you've been in the business a long time and your business is stagnant, don't waste time trying to resurrect yesterday's performers. Look for new people. It can be hard when someone you have high hopes for doesn't live up to expectations, but you must invest the bulk of your time in your top performers. They are your future leaders. So let results do the talking and work with your producers.

Allowing yesterday's fading stars to dominate your time is a losing game. Your team members deserve role models who are actively working, and you send the wrong message by giving influence or accolades to people who are no longer producing. Find other ways to show your appreciation to former contributors.

You may notice the people who are doing the least are making the most noise. But there are only two ways to fail in direct selling. The first is not doing enough; the second is doing the wrong things. If they're willing to work and willing to learn, your team members will triumph. If they're not, nothing you do will make a difference.

By teaching your recruits to function independently you'll equip them to pass along their skills and experience to their own recruits. Your example will be compounded many times over as it filters all the way down through your organization.

CHAPTER TWELVE

Embrace a Wide Range of Personalities

Learn to walk in other people's shoes.
—MARY CHRISTENSEN

In a traditional business environment, we gravitate to jobs that best match our personalities. Drivers assume leadership roles, analytical thinkers crunch the numbers, extroverts choose sales, and so it goes.

Direct selling embraces a wide range of personalities, and we must perform a multitude of tasks to grow our businesses, from sales and service to leadership and administration. Our personality determines which tasks we enjoy and which ones we don't. It indicates which tasks we are most likely to perform well and those that will take more effort. It defines how we approach each task.

Through a greater awareness of your own personality you can utilize your strengths and minimize your shortcomings to become a better business builder, leader, and manager. By understanding the different personalities in your organization you can draw out their unique talents and help them overcome their limitations.

I introduced a simple way to identify distinct personality types in my book *Be a Recruiting Superstar*. I compared different personalities to the characteristics of well-known birds to help direct sellers connect and communicate with a wide range of prospects. The same simple system will help you mentor the diverse personalities within your organization.

The majority of people fall into one of these personality groups:

★ Extroverted Peacocks
★ Conservative Doves
★ Social Robins
★ Cautious Wrens
★ Power-Seeking Eagles
★ Rational Owls
★ Unconventional Ostriches
★ Restrained Swans

Clues to our personality are written in the way we speak and how we listen when others are speaking. Our dress style, body language, and facial expressions reveal our inner selves. So does the car we drive, where we live, and how we furnish our homes.

More obvious signs are revealed by the way we respond to different situations. Stressful situations intensify our personality traits, and social situations highlight our differences.

Each personality is driven by a different motivation:

★ Peacocks are driven by a need for attention and recognition
★ Doves are driven by a need to contribute and be valued
★ Robins are driven by a need for approval and acceptance
★ Wrens are driven by a need for security and survival
★ Eagles are driven by a need for status and power
★ Owls are driven by a need for knowledge and understanding
★ Ostriches are driven by uncertainty and indecision
★ Swans are driven by personal growth

In social situations, we're naturally drawn to those with similar personality traits. We click instantly with some people, feel comfortable around others, and work harder to connect with a few. In business we don't have the luxury of picking and choosing our associates. We must bond with all personality types.

SELF-ASSESSMENT PERSONALITY TEST

Your honest answers to the following questions will reveal your personality. Each question has eight possible answers. Circle the letter next to the one that best describes you. You can select more than one answer to any question, and if none of the options fit exactly, select the closest one.

The questionnaire is a lighthearted one. Go with your first instinctive response and try not to overanalyze the questions.

1. My ideal job involves:

a. People contact/variety/ stimulation

b. Helping others/doing something worthwhile

c. Working with a great team/ being appreciated

d. Job security/prepared to do anything if the pay is right

e. Responsibility/high salary/ benefits

f. Autonomy/problem solving

g. Anything as long as it's not too demanding

h. A chance to prove myself/ good training

2. At a formal event I am:

a. The most colorful

b. Passing plates to the over-worked server

c. Taking lots of photos

d. Wishing I were somewhere else

e. Directing the conversation

f. Wanting to discuss current events

g. Trying to cover the stain I made on the tablecloth

h. Hoping I'm using the right fork

3. This best describes my finances:

a. My credit cards are maxed out

b. Money doesn't buy happiness

c. As long as I can pay the bills . . .

d. I have a six-month emergency fund

e. People who say money doesn't buy happiness don't know where to shop

f. I carefully check my bank statements

g. I try not to think about money

h. I am a saver

4. My approach to shopping is:

a. I consider it retail therapy

b. I enjoy choosing gifts

c. I prefer to shop with a friend

d. I never make an impulse purchase

e. I expect good service

f. I can calculate the tax in my head

g. I tag along if others are going to the mall

h. I love to window-shop

5. This one best describes my closet:

a. Overflowing

b. Soft colors and pastels

c. Trendy

d. Functional

e. Looks like an upscale fashion store

f. Organized

g. Don't open the door, that's all I can say

h. I'd love a fashion makeover

6. This set of words describes me:

a. Sociable, spontaneous, enthusiastic, impulsive, talkative

b. Caring, dependable, conservative, kind, capable

c. Optimistic, cheerful, accepting, cooperative, undemanding

d. Steady, hard-working, cautious, resourceful, determined

e. Competitive, powerful, confident, ambitious, driven

f. Organized, analytical, curious, rational, methodical

g. Relaxed, carefree, forgetful, disorganized, friendly

h. Sensitive, shy, apprehensive, emotional, hopeful

7. About my school days:

a. I was a cheerleader

b. I helped organize the prom

c. I still keep in touch with school friends

d. I kept pretty much to myself

e. I ran for class president

f. My favorite subjects were math and technology

g. I wish I could live them all over again

h. I almost joined the drama group but lost my nerve

8. In a high-rise building, my "elevator etiquette" is:

a. I often forget to hit the button for my floor

b. I offer to push the buttons for others

c. If there's a crowd, I squash up so more people can get in

d. If the elevator is full, I wait for the next one

e. I make use of the time to text or talk on my cell phone

f. I count the floors as the elevator rises

g. I often forget what floor I'm meant to be on

h. I secretly study the other passengers

9. My dream home is:

a. A place where friends gather

b. A peaceful place

c. A place with good neighbors

d. Away from the suburbs

e. A show home in the best area

f. One I can afford

g. Anyplace, as long as the rent's cheap . . .

h. A place I can be proud of

10. My idea of fun is:

a. A night out with friends

b. Joining in with whatever someone has planned

c. Facebook, chatting on the phone, texting

d. A quiet night in front of the television

e. Competitive sports, working out

f. Video games

g. Going with the flow

h. Dinner and a movie

11. About my driving . . .

a. I can charm my way out of a ticket

b. I'm a careful driver

c. I am happy to carpool

d. I try not to rely on my car

e. I speed up when the light turns yellow

f. I combine trips to save gasoline

g. I'll be driving again as soon as my car is repaired

h. I'm anxious in heavy traffic

12. My ideal vacation is:

a. Sun, sand, shopping

b. Visiting my sister

c. A family reunion

d. Hiking in the wilderness

e. First-class all the way

f. A different cultural experience

g. A road trip

h. A romantic getaway

When you've answered every question, add up how many of each letter you circled. Your dominant personality is the one you circled most. The higher your score in that category, the more intense your behavioral characteristics are. The next highest score indicates your secondary traits. It's the combination of traits that gives each of us our unique character.

>*Mostly A's indicate an expressive Peacock*
>*Mostly B's indicate an empathetic Dove*
>*Mostly C's indicate a friendly Robin*
>*Mostly D's indicate a guarded Wren*
>*Mostly E's indicate an ambitious Eagle*
>*Mostly F's indicate an analytical Owl*
>*Mostly G's indicate a idiosyncratic Ostrich*
>*Mostly H's indicate a timid Swan*

If you've scored close to equal numbers of two letters, you're a hybrid. For example, equal B's and C's indicate a balance of Dove/Robin; equal B's and F's a balanced Dove/Owl.

If your scores are uneven, the higher number indicates your dominant personality and the lower number your secondary personality traits. If you circled mostly E's and a few F's, you're an Eagle with Owl tendencies. If you circled mostly F's and one or two D's, you're an Owl with Wren characteristics.

Some personalities cannot be blended, as the motivations that drive them are contradictory. If you're a driven Eagle, your thoughtful Dove traits will be overwhelmed by your ambition. If you're a social Peacock, you can't also be a reclusive Wren. Robins are followers, so they cannot also be power-seeking Eagles.

If you've circled several answers for each question, there's every chance you're a Peacock.

Now let's look at the behaviors associated with each personality.

Peacocks
The most colorful of all personalities, Peacocks are enthusiastic, spontaneous, and passionate. They follow their instincts, radiate warmth, and make friends easily.

Peacocks are drawn to the limelight. They talk often, speak quickly, and sometimes embellish a story for effect.

Extreme Peacocks will do anything to attract attention.

Doves

The most sensitive of all personalities, Doves are caring, nurturing, and kind.

Doves bring harmony to any group. They're thoughtful, considerate, and tolerant of all viewpoints. They'll turn away from a disagreement rather than hurt someone's feelings.

Extreme Doves often sacrifice their own goals to serve others, and are vulnerable to being taken advantage of.

Robins

The most stable of all personalities, Robins place high value on relationships.

They're accommodating and adaptable and are easily swayed by the opinions of others. They're not initiators, they love company, and they are highly responsive to peer pressure. They may have a tendency to gossip.

Extreme Robins are overly dependent on other people's opinions.

Wrens

The most reserved of all personalities, Wrens are as resourceful as they are hardworking. Ultimate survivors, they'll do whatever it takes to provide for the people they care about.

Wrens do not trust easily and prefer to operate alone or in small numbers.

Extreme Wrens are overly suspicious of other people's motives.

Eagles

The most driven of all personalities, Eagles live to win. Confident, ambitious, and assertive, they won't stop until they get what they want.

Eagles know how to turn on the charm to get their own way, but lack of tact and patience can be their downfall.

Extreme Eagles will trample over others without conscience to achieve their goals.

Owls

The most observant of all personalities, Owls are drawn to facts, figures, and detail. They're sincere and reliable, if sometimes a little stubborn.

Patient, methodical thinkers, they enjoy problem solving and delving deep into issues that interest them.

Extreme Owls are unyielding perfectionists.

Ostriches

The most unconventional of personalities, Ostriches are a little hazy when it comes to determining their niche in life.

Intelligent, imaginative, and entrepreneurial, they get by on the strength of their affable personalities.

Extreme Ostriches tend to be misfits.

Swans

The most emotional of personalities, Swans have big dreams but believe they're somehow unworthy or unqualified to realize them.

Their lack of confidence often stems from being let down or put down by others and they're easily hurt by perceived slights that others would brush off.

Extreme Swans are timid and withdrawn.

WORKING WITH THE DIFFERENT PERSONALITIES

The more successful you are at bringing out the best in every team member, the more profitable your business will be. By learning to adapt to personality differences you'll be better able to help your team members work to their strengths, coax out their potential, and minimize attitudes and behaviors that are holding them back.

Social Peacocks

Motivate your high-maintenance Peacocks with enthusiasm and excitement. Peacocks are highly responsive to recognition and rewards, but are easily distracted and need constant stimulation to stay focused.

Peacocks are natural networkers. Encourage them to take advantage of every timesaving tool available so they can spend their time at the front line, where they are the most effective.

Peacocks have short attention spans and may lack discipline when it comes to routine tasks, so make sure you teach them the power of following up.

Peacocks can be drama queens (or kings), and make a big deal out of small concerns. Encourage them to solve problems by focusing on the issue, instead of making it personal. Help them resolve conflict by putting themselves in the other person's shoes.

Sensitive Doves

Motivate your conservative Doves by making them feel valued. Doves have huge potential to grow when they believe in their cause and have the right support. Take it slowly, as Doves need time to accept new ideas.

You can count on your Doves to follow through on their promises, but don't take their contribution for granted; they need to be appreciated, too. A personal call or note will carry more weight than a text or e-mail.

Help Doves overcome their fear of taking advantage of others by reminding them of the value they offer in their products, host rewards, and business opportunities.

Make sure your Dove leaders are not doing too much for their people at the expense of their personal activity.

Adaptable Robins

Motivate your undemanding Robins with praise and encouragement. Robins thrive on direction. Set a target and they'll aim for it. Set an example and they'll follow it.

Robins are steady, dependable team members whose performance will depend largely on the dynamics that exist in your group. They're highly responsive to peer pressure and will work hard to keep up with other team members.

Robins have a tendency to look for support when the going gets tough rather than solve their problems themselves. Robins don't like to be left out and they're easily slighted, so make sure they always feel included.

They'll need gentle persuasion to stretch beyond their comfort zones and take on leadership responsibilities.

Reserved Wrens

Motivate your cautious Wrens by giving them time to adjust to the social nature of their job. Wrens may be slow to embrace direct selling but when they do, they will display an impressive resourcefulness. Once they commit, they'll work tirelessly to achieve the results they want.

Wrens need little outside stimulation to meet the goals they set for themselves, and their initiative may surprise you.

Independent thinkers, Wrens prefer to operate under their own rules, so give them plenty of space. They withdraw when pressure is applied or when someone oversteps their boundaries. Never let them down, as they don't forgive easily.

Wrens are distrustful of too much emotion and uncomfortable being singled out in public. Save the effusive praise for your Robins and Peacocks.

Commanding Eagles

Motivate your ambitious Eagles with tangible rewards and trophies they can display as symbols of their success. Eagles are the most confident and motivated of all personalities. They thrive on competition. Give them a challenge, especially one with status attached, and they'll go for it.

Eagles are ego-driven and cope easily with situations others may find stressful, so set them on a leadership path from the start. If they don't see results quickly they'll move to a new challenge without a second thought.

They like to get their own way, and their raw ambition can be overwhelming, so don't allow Eagles to make excessive demands on your time.

Although they're highly charismatic, Eagles can turn the charm on and off at will and are less affected by confrontation than other personalities. Make sure their need to compete doesn't create conflict within the team.

Methodical Owls

Motivate your methodical Owls with substantiated facts, figures, and data. Once they understand the numbers you won't have to remind them of the need to be consistent or persistent.

You can count on your Owls to be reliable performers and not miss deadlines for incentives or bonus payments. Just make sure they don't become so bogged down in detail that they don't get around to doing anything.

Owls may need help with people skills, as their obsession with detail can come at the expense of relationships. Help them understand that not everyone will share their fascination with the finer points of the compensation plan or endless research findings about the products.

Encourage Owls who aspire to leadership to loosen up a little and embrace a less pedantic approach.

Motivate your Owls with patience and guidance.

Unfocused Ostriches

Ostriches are inattentive. Monitor them closely or there's every chance they'll miss out on a bonus payment or reward because they misunderstood or misread the fine print.

Give them short-term rather than long-term goals. They can wander off course or lose focus, so keep a close watch on their progress.

Cultivate a sense of humor and try not to become frustrated when things go awry. Ostriches are not problem solvers, and would rather avoid an issue than deal with it.

Their affable personalities make them popular team members, but don't be surprised when they turn up at the right place at the wrong time or the wrong place at the right time.

Ostriches need to be able to lead themselves before they can hope to lead a team.

Emotional Swans

Motivate your Swans with empathy and encouragement. Give them a chance to prove themselves, as they'll work hard to live up to your expectations. When they succeed they'll become living proof that this business can change lives.

Swans sometimes allow pressure to overwhelm them, and they may agonize about setbacks long after others have moved on. Encourage them to be as kind to themselves as they are to others.

Swans will flourish if they can find the right mentor, and when they succeed they'll be as generous at mentoring others as you were to them.

Every fully fledged Swan automatically becomes an inspiring role model for the next generation of Swans waiting in the wings for their chance to shine.

IT TAKES ALL KINDS TO MAKE A TEAM

The lesson is to embrace diversity in your organization, as the benefits you'll gain far outweigh the effort you'll make to adapt to the unique personalities in it. A diverse team will produce better results, and everyone benefits from a broader range of outlook and talents.

The bigger your organization, the more diverse your team will become. You're almost certain to have team members who are as delightful as others are demanding. You can expect to get doers and ditherers. Some team members will be difficult.

Influential leaders embrace everyone in their organization, both high and low maintenance—and still manage to keep their sanity intact.

CHAPTER THIRTEEN

Turn Your Shining Stars into Superstars

Make it your mission to create leaders, not followers.
—MARY CHRISTENSEN

T he richest reward any direct selling leader will receive is being the catalyst for a team member's success. No financial compensation will eclipse the satisfaction you'll gain from helping others achieve their goals.

The ultimate success in direct selling is to pass on your skills, and that's why the ultimate rewards go to those who do. The income you earn as an elite leader will transform your life. And seeing your team members promote up the plan, enjoy their first incentive trip, attend their first leadership conference, or receive an award will always be the greatest gift of leadership.

Commit to promoting leaders by implementing a leadership program that will give every Shining Star in your organization the best chance of becoming a Superstar.

A dedicated support program for your top performers will empower and equip them to independently lead their own teams. By duplicating your leadership program they'll promote their top performers, and your organization will develop the depth it needs to sustain success.

Even if you're a new or aspiring leader you can start a leadership program. Every elite leader starts with her first leader, and with your program in place you can concentrate on identifying your first Shining Star to work with. It only takes one to step up and you're in business. As your team grows, and more Rising Stars emerge, your leadership program will grow.

If you feel that a full-blown leadership program is premature, start by forming a Travel Club. The purpose of the Travel Club is to achieve the company incentive trip. Any team member who achieves the trip will be well on the way to becoming a breakaway leader. You can label your leadership program any way you like, so let your creative juices flow.

However you position it, a leadership program should offer advanced training and support for team members who demonstrate the desire and the potential to become leaders. Entry to it should be based on two key performance criteria.

The first of these is *past performance*. Your program will have credibility and substance if the only entry qualification is performance. That also makes it easy to establish eligibility, because the only measure of performance is results.

Inviting team members to participate prematurely will devalue the program. If you have team members who are eager to participate but fall short of the required past performance criterion, invite them to earn a place by improving their results.

The second is *continuing growth*. The purpose of the program is to promote leaders, so there must be an expectation of ongoing results. The more committed the participants are, the more successful the program will be. That's where the magic of momentum kicks in. The more successful the program is, the more aspiring leaders it will attract.

Design your leadership program to parallel your company's compensation plan. The compensation plan, and the incentives that accompany it, are designed to drive behavior and reward results. What makes the plan such a powerful leadership tool is that there's no uncertainty involved. Everyone knows exactly what he or she will receive when they reach each level.

By aligning your performance expectations to the compensation plan you'll have measurable targets to aim for and tangible rewards to keep your aspiring leaders motivated.

As soon as you identify your Shining Stars, even if they are new to the business, invite them to participate in your leadership program. Your sprinters will reveal themselves early by achieving all the Fast Start Rewards.

Your long-distance runners may take longer to find their stride. Consistent performance is key to reaching the upper echelons of the plan, and many slow but steady performers wake up to the benefits of leadership after months or years of minimal performance. Never write anyone off. Goals and circumstances can change in a heartbeat.

An invitation into the leadership program will act as powerful recognition when you say:

- ★ *I'm impressed by what you're achieving, and you're definitely leadership material. I'm inviting you into my leadership program.*
- ★ *You have leader written all over you, and I have exciting news. Your results for the last two months qualify you for our Shining Star Program.*
- ★ *You've only been in the business three months but your performance has been amazing. This may come as a surprise—I'm moving you into my Top Achievers Club. You already have your first two team members, so there's no reason to wait.*

EIGHT STEPS TO KEEP YOUR LEADERSHIP PROGRAM FOCUSED AND SIMPLE

Just as you create a realistic roadmap for all new recruits, plan a clear step-by-step format for your leadership program.

1. Start developing every new aspiring leader by conducting a one-on-one Moving Up interview that establishes goals and expectations. Don't rely on the goals expressed during the Welcome interview. We should review and refresh our goals every time something changes, and what bigger change can there be than deciding to step up to leadership?

Outline the requirements and rewards of the next two levels of the compensation plan. Don't alarm or overload your Shining Stars by moving too fast. By focusing on the next two levels you reinforce the concept that leadership is not a destination, but a continuum. Always keep your focus close. When they achieve one level, they'll be ready to set their sights on the next.

Confirm their commitment to meeting key performance targets for personal and team performance. Weekly targets work better than monthly targets because they allow you to more easily monitor performance and provide instant feedback and training.

Make sure your Shining Stars understand the importance of consistent effort. A lack of consistency can lead to problems down the road. If their performance is erratic they won't become the role models their teams deserve.

2. Schedule regular leadership training to drive momentum. The format, location, and timing of training will depend on the needs and circumstances of your aspiring leaders, how many are involved, and whether your company or upline leaders run leadership training programs you can tap into.

3. Allocate the last week of each month to review the month and finalize planning for the next. Don't neglect the basics. If your aspiring leaders don't have bookings they will not promote. Encourage them to collaborate on special events such as fund-raisers, trade shows, opportunity meetings, and team training days. Keep everyone inspired and motivated by publicly applauding achievements.

4. Leadership training doesn't need to be complicated. The principles used in basic training also apply to leadership training:

★ *What do they need to know now?*
★ *What do they need to do now?*

Don't reinvent the wheel by writing your own materials. This book is a comprehensive guide to building, leading, and managing a successful direct selling business, and each chapter is a complete leadership tutorial. Blend your company leadership manual with this book to ensure that your new leaders have a replicable system to follow when they start working with their own Shining Stars.

Leverage your time and cultivate a culture of independence by requiring program participants to read each chapter of this book and the company leadership manual before training, and to come prepared with questions and comments. The less time you spend teaching content, the more time you'll have for coaching.

5. *Training is worthless if it's not followed by action.*   End each tutorial by asking participants to write an action plan based on what they learned.

The action plan must address these two questions:

★ *What were the key lessons I learned from this tutorial?*
★ *How will I apply them to my business?*

Make sure their answers are specific. *I'm going to stop procrastinating* may sound impressive, but it's too vague to hold your aspiring leader accountable.

I'm going to make my ten calls between 9:00 AM and 10:00 AM every day is a specific commitment you can measure.

An effective way to ensure that the action plan has substance is to ask every participant to answer these questions:

★ *What will I start doing?*
★ *What will I stop doing?*

6. *Commitment and accountability are the keys to leadership.* Schedule a weekly one-on-one progress and planning phone call with each participant to review the previous week and agree on action steps for the next. Encourage each aspiring leader to treat the business like a business by pre-scheduling the calls for the same time every week and asking the person to call you. By calling the participants you put them in the passenger seat, and leaders have to perform at the wheel.

7. *Although you'll make yourself as available and accessible as possible, the purpose of your leadership program is to develop independently functioning leaders.* When they ask for help, don't jump in too quickly with solutions. Ask questions instead:

★ *How do you think this should be handled?*
★ *What have you decided is the best course of action?*
★ *How have you attempted to solve this problem so far?*

Sometimes all your aspiring leaders will need is a chance to talk through the issue with you.

8. *You may face a situation in which someone in the program stalls before promoting up the plan.* Every situation will be different, but allowing Falling Stars to continue in the program defeats its purpose. The best way to handle those who stop performing is to give them a break, with an invitation to return when they can commit to the time and expectations involved.

Being too relaxed with those who fall short of expectations will demoralize those who are working hard. By setting the bar high and not compromising the program, you'll demonstrate strong leadership.

EXPAND YOUR PROGRAM

As the number of Rising Stars increases, your income and skills will increase, and you can enhance the program with additional activities, resources, and benefits.

Give your Shining Stars greater involvement in planning and presenting at team meetings. There's no better way to ease them into leadership than with opportunities to take frontline roles as organizers, hosts, and presenters.

Recognize and reward them at exclusive social events.

Give them a taste of the lifestyle they'll enjoy when they promote higher up the plan. What better way to keep them motivated than:

★ Room upgrades at the national convention
★ Front-row seating, recognition, and a small gift at every team event
★ A "maid for a day" cleaning service
★ A special meal at an upscale restaurant
★ Unexpected gifts such as a voucher to a favorite store
★ Exclusive business accessories

Don't stop the leadership program when your Rising Stars become Superstars. Although some leaders will be ready to run their own programs, there's much to be gained by cooperating on future programs and initiatives.

A team conference at which all your leaders bring their teams together for a dynamic program of training, fun, inspiration, and recognition will have a powerful effect on your business. By pooling your time, resources, skills, and finances, your event can be on a grander scale.

An invitation onto your executive council or advisory board will give your highest-performing leaders an opportunity to collaborate on training programs, opportunity meetings, and special events. Make it an honor and a privilege to be invited by selecting your panel members according to the contribution they make.

Give your highest-achieving leaders the opportunity to take a break from their businesses to refresh, recharge, and reenergize themselves to move onward and upward. An annual Top Leaders' retreat in an exotic location, such as a golf resort or luxury spa, is the perfect way to blend business, networking, playing, and pampering.

If they're not enjoying time out, the whole point of building a profitable business evaporates.

CHAPTER FOURTEEN

Build Team Spirit

Make it easy for people to join and hard for them to leave.
—MARY CHRISTENSEN

The reason people join your team will not be the reason they stay. They'll join because they love the products, the income opportunity, or you. They'll stay because they feel they belong.

The strongest foundation you can build for your business is relationships. The closer the relationships you have with your team the happier they'll be, the longer they'll stay, and the harder it will be for them to leave. If their involvement is all about the products, they'll leave when they have what they need, or when they fall in love with other products. If it's only about the money, they'll leave when they hit a rough patch. If they're building bonds with you and other team members, leaving will not be a decision they make lightly.

Elite leaders make sure the cost of leaving is greater than the cost of staying. They work hard to make their people feel welcome and included. If people find themselves wondering *Is this business right for me?* or *Am I right for this business?* the next thought should be *But I don't want to leave!*

This aspect of leadership is too important to leave to chance. If you take care of your people, they'll take care of your business. Make relationships a key component of your business, and make sure everyone knows you value them as people, not just as producers. Your Distributors are people with real lives. Their personal lives will be closely entwined with their business lives. Elite leaders make it their business to know what's going on in both.

I recently relocated to a new area and wanted to join a club. As two similar clubs operated in the area I decided to visit both of them before choosing which one I would join.

At the first club I introduced myself to the organizer, but she was busy and could give me only a few seconds of her time. Although the other members were friendly, I didn't have a chance to talk to the organizer again. I waited for a while after the meeting ended, but she was chatting with a group of regular members.

At the second club I was greeted warmly, and when the meeting started, the organizer introduced me to everyone. At the end of the meeting she thanked me for coming, gave me a schedule of upcoming meetings, and said, "I hope we see you next week."

It took me all of two seconds to decide which club I wanted to join.

This is such a simple concept. People go where they feel welcome, and they stay where they feel engaged and included. Although you have to allocate the bulk of your time to new people and producers, don't neglect your smaller players. It doesn't take a huge effort to make everyone feel involved and appreciated.

Do it because it's the right thing to do, and because you never know when circumstances may change. Small players may turn on to the business at any time, and the chance of that happening is greater if they're plugged into the energy and enthusiasm generated by other team members.

CREATING TEAM SPIRIT

Make every team member feel included and appreciated by making team-building activities part of your annual program.

* Start each year by inviting everyone to share their goals with the team. That will help inspire anyone who has not yet finalized a goal to formulate one. Keep the goals alive by referring to them often. When a team member achieves a goal, recognize it individually and celebrate the achievement as "one for the team."
* Collective goals strengthen relationships. The annual incentive trip is the perfect opportunity to unite the team with one dream. When the location is announced, host an event themed to the destination and rally everyone to commit to achieving it.
* Team meetings are the ideal place to strengthen team spirit and keep your smaller producers connected. See Chapter 17 for tips on how to run magical meetings that will inspire even your smallest players.
* Keep everyone in the loop with a weekly team e-mail that shares breaking news about products, incentives, and initiatives.
* Interact with your team on Facebook. A dedicated team page will encourage your team to interact with you and each other, and it's the ideal medium for sharing news and views, information and ideas, recognition and rewards. Facebook takes a fraction of the time it takes to compile a team newsletter, and the news will spread faster.
* Ensure that team members always have something to look forward to. Whether it's the national convention, a team get-together, the launch of a new catalog, or an

impending incentive, keep anticipation levels high. Keep them focusing forward. When one milestone is reached, be ready to promote the next. When there's never a dull moment few people will have the time to leave, let alone the inclination.

★ Make the national convention a key event in your calendar and, as early as possible, encourage everyone to budget the time and the cost to attend. Most of your team will need advance notice to arrange the time off or book babysitters. Plus, early-bird registrations are cheaper, and it makes more sense to earmark a few dollars each month to cover flight and accommodation costs than to try to come up with a lump sum at the eleventh hour.

★ Attend the national convention as a team, eat meals together, and sit together for the general sessions. The convention can be an overwhelming experience for newcomers, so take extra care to ensure that first timers are looked after. Plan at least one team get-together on a free night.

★ Strengthen your team's identity with matching costumes or colors when you attend corporate events. Small steps can make a big impact on team morale.

KEEPING TEAM MEMBERS ENGAGED

To celebrate the launch of my book *Be a Party Plan Superstar* I toured America and Australia presenting party plan workshops. I was impressed at how many teams arrived together, sat together, and made a big impression when they were introduced. Many arranged to arrive early and share a meal before the workshop. Others planned get-togethers afterward.

Many successful leaders canceled their regular team training and encouraged their people to attend my workshop instead. However, they didn't abandon them. Some asked for reserved seating, which I was happy to arrange. Others arrived with small gifts for every team member, or encouraged everyone to wear team colors and outfits.

One top leader brought a huge group along and all of them were instantly recognizable by the large pink gerbera pinned to each person's lapel. This made it easy for her to recognize her own team members in the crowd and helped them find each other. However, her team was also spread across the country, and in many locations I spotted a big bright pink gerbera and knew immediately which team that person was with. Great leadership.

Never let an opportunity slip by to include as many of your team members as possible and in as many ways as possible. Even something as simple as a team name will boost morale, especially if you give everyone a chance to be involved by running a contest to see who can come up with the best name.

Here are a few more ways you can foster team spirit:

★ Encourage everyone to hold an open house during a specific week to showcase new products to customers, hostesses, and prospects. Hold a brainstorming meeting before the open house week to pool ideas. Review results afterward so everyone can benefit from lessons learned and apply them when they plan their next open house.

★ Bring your team together to host a booth at an expo, trade show, or craft fair. They'll be forging stronger bonds as they drum up new business.

★ Working for a community cause is a great way to strengthen team spirit. Adopt a local charity, or arrange a working bee for a family or business such as a daycare in need. Deliver small gifts to a senior center or assisted living facility. Not only will it remind team members to be grateful for what they have, it will also give a wonderful lift to others.

★ Run team phone-athons, book-athons, or sponsor-athons when extra effort is needed to achieve an incentive.

Reward highest attendance, sales, bookings, and sponsoring to spur on the more competitive members of the team, and add to the fun with a few impromptu and noncompetitive awards. Nothing works quite the same as laughter when it comes to balancing out the disappointment of a less-than-spectacular result. Let me share my own personal experience with that.

The organization I joined to improve my speaking skills was Toastmasters. Many awards and trophies are presented for excellence, but the one that created the most buzz at my club was the bone award.

The bone was painted neon pink. At the end of every meeting it was awarded to the person who made the biggest gaffe.

I stumbled many times and was often the person who took the neon pink bone home. The silliness of the award helped ease the frustration of being less confident and polished than I wanted to be.

In fact I won the pink bone so often that it spent a lot of time on my mantel at home. One night I didn't take it home, and the next morning my four-year old son came to tell me, "Mommy, the pink vase has gone."

★ Not every initiative has to be a grand one. Small steps, such as letting phone callers know you're happy to hear from them, make a difference. Never give the impression that you're stressed or busy. No one will feel slighted when you ask to call back at a more convenient time if you preface your request with a friendly greeting.

★ The most powerful emotion is love. The opposite of love is indifference. No one wants to be ignored or excluded. We all want to feel special. When you single out someone and say, *It's a special meeting next month and I really want you to be there*, you can almost guarantee they'll show up.

When someone misses a meeting and you call to say, *We had a great meeting but we missed you,* you dramatically increase the likelihood that they'll be at the next one.

★ Remember and acknowledge important occasions in your team members' lives. Never be too busy to send a card on a birthday, inquire about a family member, or remember that a child excelled at school. No one walks away from people they feel close to on a personal level.

★ A time-effective way to ensure that you're keeping up with events in your team members' lives is to circulate a simple questionnaire at the start of the year, asking them to share their personal and business highlights of the past year. You can guarantee it will make interesting reading and reveal news you may have missed.

★ Demonstrate that you are a team player by sharing the spotlight at every opportunity. When you achieve any leadership recognition, acknowledge the contribution your team has made publicly, and take time afterward to thank each person privately. Team achievements help generate one of the most priceless assets your business can have, and that's team pride.

The bottom line is that few direct sellers make a conscious decision to leave the business. Most simply drift away. The closer the bonds you build with them and the closer the bonds they have with each other, the more likely it is that they'll stick around, through good times and bad.

If you genuinely care about your people, you'll do all you can to create an environment where everyone feels engaged, appreciated, and happy.

You'll decide what kind of team you would like to belong to, and you'll create that team. You'll decide what kind of leader you would like to have, and you'll be that leader.

PART THREE

Business
Leadership

Treat your business like a business.
—MARY CHRISTENSEN

CHAPTER FIFTEEN

Be a Proactive Leader

Always be in a position to influence results.
—MARY CHRISTENSEN

Your income is based on results, so you can't afford to take a laissez faire approach to business. The more hours everyone within your organization works, and the more productively they work those hours, the more you—and they—will earn. By monitoring team performance weekly you'll be positioned to take the appropriate action at the appropriate time to maximize everyone's income.

Think of it as "no surprises" leadership. When you know what's happening you'll know where your attention is needed.

End-of-month management is ineffective management. Every abandoned customer, canceled appointment, party without forward bookings, or prospect who starts out interested but then says no to the business is a missed income opportunity for you and for the team member who caused the problem.

Consider these all-too-common scenarios:

★ In the last month of the promotion, a team member miscalculates the sales he needs to earn a fully paid vacation. His disenchantment causes him to lose interest in his business.

* A new recruit forgets to place an order by the deadline for a Fast Start Reward. It's a disappointing start to a promising business.

* An emerging leader is let down by a team member who promises to place an order but subsequently decides to hold the order over until next month. Instead of celebrating her promotion, you're commiserating with a disheartened team member.

* A promising new team member doesn't sponsor in the first three months but you don't investigate the reason, nor do you offer support. After three months he drifts away, and with him go all his contacts. After all the effort you put into sponsoring him, you're back to square one.

Most of these failures can be avoided with hands-on leadership. Problems don't go away, but people do when they're not getting the help they need to get results. Make your actions count by monitoring and managing performance on your team.

You cannot be proactive and disorganized at the same time. Put systems in place to support the most productive aspects of your business and actively work those systems.

TEN WAYS TO BE A HANDS-ON LEADER

A little advance planning will go a long way toward making your programs run smoothly and effectively.

1. Develop a structured calendar. It shows you take your business seriously and makes it easier to plan effective training and support programs.

Circulate your schedule a year in advance, with dates of training meetings, team calls, expos, fairs, and fund-raisers, as well as company initiatives such as the national convention, regional meetings, and product releases.

Seek input from your breakaway leaders. By mapping the year out together you can agree when to combine activities and when to organize them separately.

Check that your schedule doesn't clash with key school dates or public holidays before you publish it.

Update the schedule every time new initiatives are announced, including qualification and travel times for incentive trips. You don't want anyone missing out because of scheduling conflicts or because you waited too long to advise them of the dates.

Once the calendar is published, avoid making unnecessary changes. Your team members deserve the certainty of a calendar they can count on. Changes lead to confusion, and confusion leads to chaos.

With everything mapped out in advance you will have a much better chance of getting your team to commit to participating:

★ *This is a big trade show, and so we work it together.*
★ *No one misses team meetings.*
★ *We go to Convention as a team.*
★ *We all host open houses every time new products are launched.*

2. Encourage smart work habits.   You don't want anyone missing out on incentives because of last-minute postponements or cancellations.

Safeguard against disappointment by suggesting team members schedule appointments and presentations early in the month. That allows ample time to rebook postponed appointments within the same month, or organize substitute activities if the appointments are canceled.

Reduce the end-of-month rush to meet company targets by running incentives that drive activity in the first half of the month.

3. Maximize your time.   Promoting leaders is the name of the game, but you can't afford to be distracted from your personal activity. Always maintain a regular schedule of personal parties, presentations, and appointments to ensure a steady flow of new people into your organization.

If your personal activity is lackluster you'll be vulnerable every time a leader promotes from your group. Regularly test your income security by subtracting the volume of your Shining Stars from your group volume. If you can easily maintain without your star performers, your income is more secure.

One of the most productive ways to juggle your personal and team responsibilities is to allocate the first half of the month to personal activity and the second half to team activity. Once you reach your personal targets you can focus on helping your team reach theirs. If you're scrambling to meet your own targets at the end of each month you won't have time to give your team members the attention they deserve.

As your business grows your workload will grow, and you can allocate your time accordingly. When you have multiple breakaway leaders it makes sense to split your time three ways:

- ★ One-third on personal activity
- ★ One-third on group activity
- ★ One-third supporting your breakaway leaders

4. Stretch your working year as far as possible.   With a little advance planning and some strategic initiatives you can start your team working early in January, avoid a long summer hiatus, and keep them working late into December.

Ensure that no one starts the new year with an empty calendar by training as early as October and November on how to get bookings in January. Support your training by running an incentive in December that rewards those who generate the most forward bookings for the following year.

Giving them a reason to work will always work better than giving them a directive to work, and the more ideas you generate, the more likely it is your team will run with them.

Encourage everyone to send thank-you cards to customers and hosts before the holidays, with a special January offer enclosed. If the offer must be redeemed in the first two weeks of the month your team will have a good reason to start making servicing calls. Reinforce your initiative by declaring January "Customer Loyalty Month."

Create fun themes for summer parties to keep the team working throughout the summer. A few examples are picnic parties, pool parties, patio parties, summer solstice parties, and mid-year Christmas parties.

One of the most basic rules of direct selling is that the more people you meet the more money you'll make. Encourage your team to combine networking with not working when they're on vacation.

Remind them to pack catalogs, brochures, and samples with their swimsuits and sunglasses and to make their products visible. The people camping next to them at the lake may be their next team members, hosts, or customers.

Hold your team meeting at the earliest possible date in September to switch everyone from vacation mode to work mode. The shorter their break, the easier it will be to mobilize them.

Recommend open houses as soon as the kids go back to school. To keep their homes from being overrun with other people's children, they can schedule their open houses to begin after the kids have been dropped off at school.

Schedule cash-and-carry sales the week before the holidays to capture last-minute sales and clear unwanted inventory.

Hold your annual team celebration after the last date for holiday orders has passed.

5. Drive performance with a mix of individual and team recognition programs. When you set a target, there will always be those who will shoot for it. Different incentives will appeal to different personalities:

- ★ Personal incentives, such as *beat your personal best* targets, will inspire highly motivated team members to keep stretching.
- ★ Team competitions for highest sales, recruits, or bookings will encourage competition between your most motivated team members.
- ★ Consistency targets will encourage and reward steady performers.

Make sure your name appears at the top of the leader board often, and encourage lively competition. Reward superior performance by saying, *The only thing I love more than achieving the top spot is when one of my team members beats me.*

6. *Track promises against performance.* At the beginning of each month, ask everyone in your personal group to call in their upcoming activity, including prospects they have in the pipeline. Record it all on a large desktop calendar, or a wall chart above your work space. If you see that bookings are below what will be needed to meet personal or team targets, start looking for ways to generate more business.

Keep an especially close eye on new people, consistent performers, and qualifying leaders. It's better to say, "That seems like a light schedule for the results you need" early in the month than to wait until it's too late to coax more activity out of them.

If you're constantly on the move you may find it easier to monitor team activity electronically, but large at-a-glance charts will make it easier to view the big picture. The clearer it is, the clearer it will be to see who needs your support.

7. *Actively work your group schedule.* Constantly check the schedule against the results flowing in and respond as soon as possible when performance exceeds or falls short of expectations.

Make encouraging calls to all new people the day they have parties scheduled, and again the next day to review results and offer coaching.

Text a positive message to experienced team members before their parties, and ask them to text their results back to you immediately afterward. Then follow up. Achievers will appreciate your congratulatory call, and the sooner you address problems the sooner you can help resolve them.

8. Don't sit on information.   Be alert and responsive to memos coming from corporate to avoid these common scenarios:

★ The company messages all leaders extending the deadline for a promotion one week. You don't read the memo until it's too late to share the news with your team. Because they don't know about it about it they don't take advantage of it.

★ The week before the holidays the company advises leaders that a popular item may run out. You decide to take no action, as it's only a few days until last holiday orders must be submitted. Your team members continue to sell the item in good faith and then when it runs out they cannot fulfill their customers' orders. They spend the week before the holidays scrambling to come up with acceptable substitutes to keep their customers happy.

★ You attend a leadership conference and garner a goldmine of great ideas. Instead of immediately sharing them with your team on a live call, you decide to type them up and circulate them. Months pass and you still have not found time to do it. Something always seems to get in the way and eventually the ideas are lost under a landslide of new information.

Forward information and ideas to your team immediately so all of them can run their businesses with minimal stress and for maximum profit.

9. Encourage idea sharing, interaction, and feedback on your team Facebook page. I often do training calls for top leaders, and the smarter ones immediately follow up with a posting about the "ah-ha moment" they experienced from the call. Every team member is inspired by something different from the training, and enthusiasm spreads through the team. After a few days the ideas translate into "I tried it and it worked" postings, and the value of the training increases.

10. Keep up with advancements, trends, and initiatives. One thing you can count on today is change, and plenty of it. The faster you adapt, the better. Nowhere does this apply more than it does with technological advancements. If you blink you'll be left behind.

Embrace changes in the company product, policies, or plan. Change can be unsettling, but it's normal for companies to modify their systems in response to market conditions. The faster you accept changes, the smoother the transition will be for your team.

Keep up with shifting demographics. Gen Y's (born between 1980 and 1994) constitute the most powerful consumer group in the world. Don't be caught napping. Actively seek out young people as customers, hosts, and prospects, because they are your future income.

The lesson is simple. When you are proactive you can drive performance, morale, and results. By helping your team members maximize their income opportunities you will maximize your income opportunities. By demonstrating proactive leadership you will set an example that every breakaway leader in your organization can emulate.

CHAPTER SIXTEEN

Work Smarter

Maximize your income by maximizing your partnerships.
—MARY CHRISTENSEN

Although the real action takes place at the front line, you still have to manage your business. The trick is to spend as little time as possible on paperwork so you'll have more time for people work. Follow these seven steps to reduce the time you spend on unproductive activity and free yourself for productive pursuits.

STEP ONE: DON'T DO ANYTHING THE CORPORATION CAN DO

Let the company take care of the back end of the business, and spend your time at the front line.

One of the greatest advantages of direct selling is that you don't have to write your own business plan. The compensation plan outlines what you must do to grow your business and rewards you every step of the way. Steer your business in the right direction by following the plan.

The incentive programs that accompany the plan are designed to reward the actions that generate income, so the team culture you need to create is that *"everyone aims for every incentive."* Keep in mind that there's no point in doubling down on incentives. When the company runs an incentive you're throwing money away by concurrently running one of your own.

Although you will sometimes run incentives to drive specific actions, avoid unnecessary expense by keeping them simple. Even if you can afford it, costly incentives will discourage team members seeking leadership status. Keep the time period for earning an incentive short. An incentive can quickly become a disincentive if team members fall behind.

Take advantage of every company initiative, including visits by corporate trainers to your area. Seize them as a break from organizing your own meeting and promote them enthusiastically. The more team members who attend, the more your business will benefit. For any key event encourage out-of-towners to carpool and split the cost of a hotel room, or ask local team members to host them.

STEP TWO: SUPPORT YOUR COMPANY 100 PERCENT

Respect the partnership you have with the corporation. You may not agree with everything it does (just as the company may not agree with everything you do), but that doesn't give you license to debate its decisions. A company with a hundred thousand Distributors has a hundred thousand clients, all with different perspectives and circumstances. Not everyone is going to be happy all of the time.

Sometimes companies make mistakes. A company that isn't willing to make bold moves or take risks will quickly become stagnant.

Don't waste your time trying to influence aspects of the business outside your control. Work on improving your own performance. You can have everything your own way when you get your own planet.

STEP THREE: DON'T DO ANYTHING YOU CAN DODGE, DISCARD, OR DELEGATE

There will never be enough hours to do everything you need to do, so don't waste time doing things you *don't* need to do. Your income is derived from selling, sponsoring, and promoting leaders, and that should tell you how to spend your time.

Don't encumber your business with complicated systems. Whether you're running it from a corner of the living room or you have the luxury of a dedicated office, make sure you're organized. A cluttered environment makes it difficult to focus. A cluttered mind makes it impossible to focus.

One party per week will pay for a lot of help. The services of an office assistant and someone to clean your home will increase your workweek. Always hire bright-eyed applicants, as they may well become your next recruits when they see how rewarding your business is.

Never put off until tomorrow what you can deal with today. Unfinished business is a liability, and delaying tasks doesn't make them any easier. Spend a few minutes tying up loose ends at the end of each day so that you can start fresh the next morning.

Don't micromanage your personal business, your breakaway leaders, or your family. Sometimes the best course of action is to do nothing.

STEP FOUR: MAKE THE MOST OF YOUR RESOURCES

You have an advantage over most small businesses in the first-class products, training, and marketing materials produced by your corporate partner. Work that advantage:

★ Don't produce your own materials, make copies to save a few dollars, or deface literature with slapdash personalization.

★ Buy the best quality business cards you can afford and use clean, contemporary graphics. Amateurish embellishments and advertising will undermine your professional image.

★ Transport your demonstration products in professional totes and refresh them often.

★ Don't allow basic skills training to swallow up time you can spend more effectively on coaching. Circulate a list of recommended books to your team members and encourage them to learn independently. Start with my books published by AMACOM:

~*Be a Network Marketing Superstar* is a step-by-step guide to building a party plan, direct selling, or network marketing business.

~*Be a Recruiting Superstar* explains how to identify, approach, and close the best prospects.

~*Be a Party Plan Superstar* is full of tips on generating higher sales, bookings, and business leads at every party or presentation.

~This current book will inspire, empower, and equip your stars to become independent leaders of their own teams.

★ Leverage your time by starting a book club in your organization. Each team member who reads just one chapter of a recommended book every week will benefit from fifty hours of independent learning over the course of a year. When your team shares questions and feedback on calls and at meetings, everyone will benefit.

STEP FIVE: MAKE YOUR PERSONAL ACTIVITY COUNT TWICE

On-the-job experience will always be more effective than formal training, so be sure to take new and inexperienced team members with you to every party. Introduce your "assistant" as a bonus for guests: *This is Samantha. You're in luck tonight as there are two of us and we can give you more personal attention.*

Your resourcefulness will yield double benefits. The more personal attention guests receive, the more they'll spend.

When you take team members to a one-on-one appointment say, *I hope you're happy for Tyler to sit in. He's just starting his business.*

STEP SIX: WORK ON YOUR WEAKNESSES

Don't squander your strengths by neglecting your weaknesses.

Perhaps you're successfully promoting leaders, but they're not promoting leaders in turn. You can look for someone to blame (*no one steps up, they're not working hard enough* . . .) or you can look for solutions.

You have to ask the tough questions before you can solve the problem:

- ★ *Do I believe in my leaders?*
- ★ *Do I let them know I believe in them?*
- ★ *Have I prepared them for leadership?*
- ★ *Is my leadership program replicable?*
- ★ *Am I stifling my leaders by being the sole star of the show?*

STEP SEVEN: TAKE CONTROL OF SETBACKS

As you build your business you'll experience setbacks. They may be small: missing out on a bonus check for lack of a few more dollars in sales, or losing a prospect at the eleventh hour.

They may be major: the evaporation of your team when you thought things were going well, the defection of a supposedly loyal consultant to a rival company, or falling short of the target that would have earned you a company car.

Setbacks will take the wind out of your sails if you let them. They are part of normal business growth. The only way to deal with them is to pick yourself up, dust yourself off, and get on with the job.

It doesn't matter what created the problem. What matters is what you do about the problem. Think:

What went wrong?
Why did it go wrong?
How will I fix it?
What will I do differently to prevent it from happening again?

By taking control of the problem you take control of the solution. Most failures come from not doing enough, or doing the wrong things. If your team has dwindled, it may be because you worked with the wrong people, or didn't introduce enough fresh talent, or your leadership skills need work. All of these problems are fixable. Seize the opportunity to find new people and resolve to become a better leader next time around.

Don't buy into negativity. Put the failure into perspective, and don't take it personally. Think *This is a failure*, not *I'm a failure*. Indulging in a giant pity party is destructive and pointless.

If you've had a major setback, remind yourself that you're not back at the starting gate. You have a wealth of skills and experiences to draw on and you're wiser from the lessons you have learned. Reset your goals and move forward. There's nothing like a fresh challenge to erase the memory of the one that didn't turn out as you'd hoped.

CHAPTER SEVENTEEN

Make Your Meetings Magical

*Nothing has more power to build team spirit
than a magical meeting.*
—MARY CHRISTENSEN

Team meetings are the ideal forum for building team pride, unity, and skills, but you can't take your team's participation for granted. Make your meetings magical and you'll have a full house. Make them miserable and you can expect a plethora of "sorry, can't make it" RSVPs.

The difference between a magical meeting and a miserable one is in the detail. It takes more effort to run a magical meeting, but the return on your investment will be greater because more team members will show up to be inspired and equipped to move their business forward.

The formula for a magical meeting is SPARKLE:

* Socializing
* Participation
* Action
* Recognition
* Knowledge
* Laughter
* Excitement

"S" STANDS FOR SOCIALIZING

Your monthly meeting should provide your team members a break from the day-to-day running of their businesses and allow them to refresh, renew, and recharge their passion for the business amongst like-minded people.

Don't rush to start the formal part of your program. Designate the start and end of every meeting as team time, and promote this as an opportunity to network and socialize.

Set up before the first team member arrives so that you're at the door ready to welcome everyone. You can enlist helpers for most aspects of the meeting, but don't delegate the meet and greet. This is one of the few chances most team members will have to talk with you face-to-face. Don't allow yourself to be monopolized by one or two people at the expense of others. Keep mixing and mingling so you can make even your smallest producers feel welcome and appreciated.

Encourage everyone to attend, even those who are doing little or nothing. At one Leadership Retreat I ran someone asked this question: "What do I do about those who turn up to every meeting but never do anything?"

Before I had a chance to answer, a brand-new leader's hand shot up. "I can answer that," she said. "I was one of those people. I enjoyed the meetings but I had a full-time job so I never really did anything. Then one day I decided to go for it."

Within three months she had reached the first level of leadership and was well on her way to the next level.

It's much better to have a full house than a meager turnout caused by making low performers feel guilty or unworthy to attend. Your regular meetings are for every team member regardless of activity levels. You never know when a meeting will inspire someone to start working.

Make sure everyone wears a name tag, including your senior people. I shudder when someone says, "I don't need a name tag. Everyone knows who I am." That's not the point. The point is to make it easy for everyone, from a brand-new team member to a casual guest, to get to know each other.

If your team is in the habit of sitting quietly, waiting for the meeting to start, get them on their feet with networking exercises. The simplest one is to hand them a list of people to find:

★ *Who is attending her first meeting?*
★ *Who traveled the farthest?*
★ *Who has recently joined the business?*
★ *Who is working two jobs?*
★ *Who has young children?*
★ *Who is attending as a guest?*
★ *Who had a record-breaking month?*

This is a golden opportunity to practice networking skills. Encourage them to ask questions:

When they find someone who is working two jobs, they should ask, "*How do you do it?*"

When they find a new team member, they should ask, "*What prompted you to join?*"

When they find someone who had a record-breaking sales month, they should ask, "*How did you make it happen?*"

When they find someone who has a full calendar, they should ask, "*How do you get appointments?*"

Make sure you're accessible and approachable when the formal part of the meeting ends. Ramp up the music and invite everyone to stay for refreshments. They'll be fired and inspired and you don't want them rushing out the door. Don't start packing up until after they leave.

"P" STANDS FOR PARTICIPATION

Evaluate the success of your meetings by how well you embrace the 80/20 rule. If you're doing 20 percent of the talking and your team is doing 80 percent, you're achieving the perfect balance.

Your meeting attendees won't check their lives at the door when they arrive, so immediately after the welcome and introductions invite everyone to "shout out" their personal or business news. This will help build team spirit and update you with what's happening in their lives. If this is generally a lively session, appoint someone to take discreet notes so you can follow up where appropriate.

Invite three people at different stages of the business to share their fifteen- to thirty-second stories at each meeting. Over a period of ten meetings thirty team members will get to practice sharing their stories, and your team will benefit from thirty different testimonials. Call all speakers before each meeting so they have time to prepare—and so you can create an additional thirty connections between you and your team members.

Encourage everyone to bring their questions and challenges to the meeting and place them in a box. Invite your Shining Stars to take turns drawing a question and answering it. Circulate the questions and answers by e-mail the next day so that nonattendees also can benefit.

Incorporate brainstorming and role-playing into every meeting. To train on how to present the products succinctly, invite everyone to share one key benefit from using them.

To improve party performance, run a segment called *Best Show*. Divide attendees into groups, assign each group a topic to discuss, and ask them to appoint a spokesperson to report back with their three best ideas. Try these topics:

★ Making the most of host coaching
★ Blending booking bids into your presentation
★ Showering guests with sponsoring sparks
★ Presenting the products persuasively
★ Overcoming objections
★ Closing confidently

If your training is on personalities, follow it with one of these exercises:

★ Circulate the Self-Assessment Personality Test found in Chapter 12. Have everyone complete it and then ask each team member to reveal her personality to the others.

★ Give each person a list of the personalities. Assign the task of finding one person who matches each personality.

★ Give everyone an empty envelope and slips of paper. Challenge them to identify as many personalities as possible. Let them move around the room asking interesting questions of as many people as they can. When they're ready, they write their guess on a slip of paper and pop it in the envelope before moving to the next person. At the end everyone can read the slips of paper in their envelope to see how others perceive them.

★ For a more intense training workout, assign senior people a personality that differs from their own and ask them to role-play that personality in a prospecting or sales situation.

Control team members who want to dominate the meeting by establishing a few meeting etiquette guidelines. Setting time frames and appointing a timekeeper to manage them is a good way to curb over-enthusiastic contributors without alienating them.

The lesson is to not be a control freak. Give everyone a chance to contribute, and involve as many as possible as presenters. No one gets bored or distracted when they're doing the talking.

Meetings are a performance, and you can't take on the director, set designer, stagehand, musician, and performer roles and expect to do a great job. Work the talent within your team to produce a winning performance.

"A" STANDS FOR ACTION

You invest a significant amount of time and energy into each meeting and you want to see results. Results come from focused actions. Before you plan your agenda ask yourself:

What do I want my team members to do as a result of this meeting?

Build the content of your meeting around the attitudes, skills, and tools that will drive the actions you want your team to take. Cultivate immediacy by ending the meeting with a challenge or incentive that encourages immediate action.

Reinforce your training by ending every meeting asking attendees to share:

★ *What was the best idea I gained from this meeting?*
★ *How will I put it into action in my business?*

Invite everyone to write a "To Do" or "Best Idea" on a sticky note to take home and put on the bathroom mirror, so it will be the first thing they see the next day.

Follow up to see who put her "Best Idea" into action on your fifteen-minute weekly team call and in your e-communications.

"R" STANDS FOR RECOGNITION

Most of us enjoy being praised. Make everyone on your team feel special by heaping on the recognition.

Track and acknowledge personal and team milestones, and make a big deal of achievements. If you value your team members you'll never be short of ways to recognize them.

New people are the most vulnerable, so single them out for special attention. If a recruit's sponsor is not attending the meeting, arrange for that person to sit with one of your empathetic doves. Make guests feel welcome by asking the people who invited them to introduce the guests and share what they admire about them.

Add variety and spice to your recognition. This "dollar in the jar" game is guaranteed to increase productivity: Take a large glass vase or jar and a wad of dollar bills to your meetings. Invite team members to share their achievements for the month and put a dollar in the jar for each one. For example, a dollar would be added for each party, for each new sign-up (another dollar if the new recruit is at the meeting), for reaching a thousand dollars or more in sales, for achieving a Fast Start Reward, or for bringing a guest.

Give each team member a raffle ticket for every dollar they "earn for the jar." For significant achievements such as beating your personal best or promoting to a new level, put ten one-dollar bills in the jar and match it with ten raffle tickets for the achiever. That sends a message that the more you do, the more chances you have to win.

At the end of the meeting, ask someone who has not yet participated to draw one ticket to reveal who takes home all the money. By stipulating that you have to "earn" at least one dollar for a chance to win, you avoid rewarding nonperformers. You may even spur team members to make an effort just for a chance to win.

"K" STANDS FOR KNOWLEDGE

A little training often will always make a greater impact than large chunks of training, so allocate a maximum of thirty minutes for formal training.

Go easy on the product information. Always train in terms of, *How will this product improve my life?* rather than giving a laundry list of facts.

An enthusiastic testimonial from a team member who has achieved an incentive will have more firepower than a PowerPoint presentation of the qualification criteria.

Break monthly targets into weekly targets to encourage immediacy.

Always express earnings in dollars rather than percentages. You can't spend a percentage.

Reinforce the earnings by showing how quickly sales can add

up. For example, if your average annual earning per auto-ship customer is $200, you'll earn $2,000 a year for every ten customers you sign up; if your average party earnings are $150, two parties a week will earn you $300.

Cultivate the talent within your team before you look for outside speakers. The occasional outside speaker will inject fresh ideas and enthusiasm into your meeting, but choose them carefully. Only invite speakers with direct selling experience, or a message that supports direct selling.

A charismatic speaker whose message is off-point could easily distract your team from the business. I have heard many horror stories of speakers whose passion for a profession such as life coaching has tempted audience members to pursue a similar path. The grass may not be greener on the other side, but you don't want your team members to find that out after they have already gone over.

"L" STANDS FOR LAUGHTER

Factor fun into every agenda. Sharing a humorous anecdote, taking a cheerful poke at the business, or presenting a lighthearted skit will make your meetings fun. If you're serious by nature, enlist extroverted team members to inject a fun element into your meetings.

Games will increase the fun factor of your meetings and teach communication and networking skills at the same time. Here are a few ideas:

★ Invite everyone to bring a toddler photo of themselves and then have the others guess who is in each one.
★ Hand out paper and ask each attendee to write something previously unrevealed about himself and then place the slip of paper in a bag. Choose an extroverted team member to read them aloud one by one as everyone tries to guess whose secret each one is.

★ Ask a few people to guess the price of a new product, average earnings of a status level, who was top seller or recruiter for the month, what their total was—before you announce it.
★ Divide into teams for a quiz-night challenge on key topics.
★ Run your training as a popular game show.

Scatter social events amongst your business meetings throughout the year so there is always something to look forward to. Make at least one meeting a family event so partners and children can join in. Everyone performs better with family support behind them, and when family members are included they are sure to lend that support.

"E" STANDS FOR EXCITEMENT

Achievements stem from excitement, and your meetings should be as inspiring as they are interesting and informative. Never hold a meeting in a drab room. A great display, exciting visuals, balloons, streamers, welcome banners, and lively music can transform even the dullest room in seconds.

Create an inspiring theme for every meeting, and align it to company initiatives such as the next incentive trip. If there are gaps in the corporate program, create your own themes.

A few inexpensive giveaways will fuel the excitement of meetings. Hand out tiaras or crowns to top performers, sashes to those in qualification for leadership, and travel gifts to anyone on track for an incentive trip.

★ ★ ★

Above all, make your meetings SPARKLE by keeping them moving along. If they're too dry, too long, or weighed down by information everyone will quickly become distracted and demotivated.

If your meetings are magical, your Distributors will attend and they will perform better because they attended. If your meetings are dull they won't show, or you'll forever be chasing after missing RSVPs.

Every meeting planner knows that the way to get people to come to their meetings is to run great meetings.

CHAPTER EIGHTEEN

Make the Most of Your E-Tools

Maximize your e-communications by blending
high tech with high touch.
—MARY CHRISTENSEN

Technology may have revolutionized your business but that doesn't mean you can be complacent. In this sophisticated business climate it's not enough to connect and communicate with your customers, prospects, and team members. You must engage, inspire, and excite them. By blending high tech with high touch you'll gain the best of both worlds.

YOUR WEBSITE

Motivate visitors to your site to purchase your products, host a party, or explore the business by incorporating these strategies into your website design:

★ Always assume that your visitors have high expectations. The more appealing your site is, the longer they'll stay and more they'll explore.

★ You have only a few seconds to grab their attention, so design your home page to make an instant impression.

★ Your website is a reflection of you, so use the same conversational style you use when you're speaking directly with your customers and prospects.

★ Lengthy blocks of text will bury your messages. Limit the number of words per page, keep your sentences short, and use bullet points to highlight key messages.

★ Photos are always more eye-catching than words. A snapshot of you and your family at Disneyland with the caption *"I achieved my goal!"* will make a greater impact than will an explanation of your vacation.

★ Make it easy for visitors to investigate your offers by scattering live links throughout your text.

★ Always ask for the sale. Sweeten the deal with a discount or a gift-with-product offer to encourage immediate action.

★ Check to be sure that your website is mobile-enabled so you can share your business wherever the opportunity arises.

E-MAIL

Just because it's an e-mail doesn't mean it can be boring. Improve the likelihood that your e-mails will be opened, read, and responded to with these tips:

★ Choose an address that is recognizable to the recipient, and easy to remember; for example, davewalker38@aol.com or nikkijones40@live.com.

★ Set the "From" field to show your name. Most of us scroll through our e-mails before deciding which ones to open. If your name is obscure you may land in the junk mail folder.

★ Don't take shortcuts with basic courtesy. Always open with the recipient's name (*Dear Nikki*) and sign off with your name (*Warm regards, David*).

★ Keep your e-mails short if you don't want them relegated to the *I'll read it later* file. Chances are your message will be buried in the avalanche of the next day's e-mails and disappear forever.

★ Make it easy for recipients to read your message. Dense text will encourage them to skim over it. Short sentences, spacing, and lots of paragraphs will make your e-mails more readable.

★ Spell check and format your e-mails. If accuracy is not your forte, compose and edit your message offline, and then paste it into your e-mail. There's no excuse for sloppiness.

★ Think twice about forwarding e-mails. If you cannot resist, clean them up first.

★ If you're cutting and pasting a business message, take a few seconds to add a personal greeting.

★ Curb your enthusiasm for embellishments. Capital letters, bold type, fancy icons, and exclamation marks are not to everyone's taste, and most will be lost anyway as your e-mail passes through different browsers and systems.

★ Don't use jargon, clichés, and abbreviations (SED instead of Senior Executive Director) unless you want to irritate your recipients. You know what your abbreviations mean, but that doesn't mean others will be able to decipher them.

★ Always update the subject line to identify the content of your e-mail. I receive hundreds of e-mails each day and open only the ones that allow me to identify the purpose of the e-mail first.

★ Write in the active tense. For example, instead of, *Do you have time in your calendar for lunch this week?* try, *Can you meet me for lunch this week?*

★ Paste live links into your message to make it easy to access your offers.

★ Add your "office hours" below your signature so that people know the best time to call you.

★ Use the flag option to save important incoming e-mails.

E-NEWSLETTERS

E-newsletters are a huge time-saver when it comes to keeping customers informed. Make the most of e-newsletters with these tips:

★ Become an enthusiastic collector of e-mail addresses. The more contacts you have, the more potential there is to generate business.

★ Don't purchase leads. If you can't create your own contacts, it's unlikely you'll be able to generate leads from public lists.

★ If your company offers a personalized newsletter that goes directly to your customers, sign up for it. Instead of creating your own content, you can use your time more effectively on following up.

★ If you create your own e-newsletter, keep it fresh and relevant. The more targeted it is, the more likely the recipients will read it.

★ Keep it short. Never feature more than one or two products or offers at a time.

★ Don't bombard your contacts with generalized messages. Create different groups for customers, hosts, team members, Shining Stars, and leaders. Tailor your communications to their specific interests and needs.

FACEBOOK

With more than a hundred million users, Facebook is clearly a powerful business tool. Ideally you should run two Facebook pages:

★ The first is an open Facebook page for your customers, hosts, and prospects. Drive your customers to your page with exclusive and impromptu offers and keep them there with tips on how to use your products. Sharing some personal news will help showcase the lifestyle you enjoy as a self-employed entrepreneur, but too many personal posts will dilute your business messages.

★ The second is a closed Facebook page for your team. This is where you and your team can exchange news, views, accomplishments, and information in a safe setting. Not only will it help to create a sense of community; it's also the fastest way to communicate important updates, provide instant recognition, and announce impromptu incentives.

WEBINARS AND CONFERENCE CALLS

Distance is no barrier to business now that you can communicate regularly and inexpensively with your team through the Internet and free phone calling.

These steps will guarantee that your team never misses your webinars, teleclasses, conference calls, and cyber-meetings:

★ Make the events exciting. You can't see your audience and they can't see you. You have to work harder to keep them enthralled. If you give them a dull experience, you'll soon be talking to an audience of none.

★ If your needs are simple, use a free service. There's no good reason to pay for anything that you can get free.

★ Schedule regular times for calls so team members can plan their week around them. Motivate your team for the week ahead with a ten-minute call on Monday morning to share breaking news, and a thirty-minute call at the start of each month to support your monthly meeting.

★ Schedule additional calls for your Shining Stars. The timing of these calls will depend on whether you're holding live meetings. I suggest a mid-month call to drive the second half of the month, and an end-of-month call to review final results and plan for the next month.

★ Remember to turn the call-waiting feature off before each call so that the flow of your call is not interrupted.

★ Avoid using a speakerphone. It's more likely to pick up background noise and produce a poor quality recording.

★ The same applies to your cell phone. If it cuts out and if you're disconnected, all attendees will be disconnected.

★ Be on every conference call or teleclass call at least five minutes prior to the start time to welcome everyone and chat informally with those who dial in early. Reintroduce yourself a few times so that new participants know who is hosting the call.

★ Encourage your team to join the live call and record it for those who can't make it, and for those who want to listen again.

★ Use FIRE to plan the agenda of your call:

"F" stands for Fun. If your calls are too dry, your audience will be folding the laundry or checking e-mails when they're supposed to be listening.

"I" stands for Inspiration. Share individual and team
success stories to inspire your team members to want
more and do more with their business.

"R" stands for Recognition. Never let an opportunity
to recognize and reward achievers slip by.

"E" stands for Education. Twenty minutes is the
maximum for training. If your call is heavy on
information no one will have the time or the
inclination to digest it.

BLOGGING

Blogging is a great way to increase your visibility and promote your
business. However, before you start blogging:

★ Make sure you have something to say.
★ Blog in small doses if you want to avoid becoming
tiresome.
★ Write from your target audience's perspective.
★ Opt out if you feel you're communicating with the wrong
people.
★ Avoid anything that may be contentious. One person
offended is one person too many.

In an uncertain world, one thing is certain. Technology will
increasingly dominate the way you communicate with your customers, prospects, team members, and corporation. Don't sabotage your success by becoming marooned in the past. Unblock
your mind and embrace the incredible advantages that new technologies offer.

If you're technologically challenged, find someone among your
family and friends to help you make the most of the social sphere.
If necessary, pay someone to teach you. A small investment in experienced advice could pay big dividends.

Don't let carelessness and laziness cancel out the advantages you gain from technological advancements. Technology gives you the best of both worlds, but you need to remember it's a tool and will only be as effective as the person operating it.

Keep in mind that just because it's new doesn't mean it's better. What works for me may not necessarily work for you. Experiment with different technologies until you establish what works and what doesn't work for your business.

While your competitors are scrambling to find high-tech ways to make their lives easier, be the high-touch leader working your e-tools to build and strengthen relationships with your customers, prospects, and team members. Make the most of e-commerce by blending high tech with high touch.

CHAPTER NINETEEN

Build Your Platform

Market your business by marketing yourself.
—MARY CHRISTENSEN

Direct selling is a relationship business, and that makes your contacts your most valuable asset. The more awareness, visibility, accessibility, and goodwill you generate within your target market, the more contacts you'll create.

TRADE SHOWS AND OTHER EVENTS

Time will always be your most precious resource, and you must use it wisely. Although you certainly want your business to have the widest possible reach, the most cost- and time-effective places to build contacts are areas surrounding your own community. Decide where you want to grow (based on how far you want to travel) and search online for trade shows, job expos, and community activities and events. You can narrow your search by entering (name of city) + Events + Vendor Applications. Local chambers of commerce, business associations, schools, preschools, kindergartens, and service clubs will also have schedules of upcoming events.

Don't be dissuaded by smaller events. The more intimate the setting, the greater your chances of standing out in the crowd.

If you offer to sponsor the event you may have it all to yourself. This will be especially effective if the event relates to your products; for example, sponsoring a beauty pageant if you represent beauty products or a sporting event if you're in the nutrition business.

The earlier you start planning, the more negotiating power you'll have when it comes to securing discounted rates and a high traffic position for your booth. Increase your visibility by offering to donate a gift to the first fifty people through the door in exchange for your name on the program. Make sure winners have to come to your booth to collect their gifts. Gifts to anonymous winners give you zero chances to make a connection.

Think outside the box. Event organizers are almost certain to be fully engaged in their community, so build strong relationships with them. They may turn out to be your most valuable contacts.

Plan your booth to create maximum visibility. Corner sites and those close to entry doors and catering stations are the highest-traffic areas. Make it easy for visitors to enter by avoiding barriers between you the crowd. Position your display to one side or at the back so that you can be center stage, ready to engage everyone who strolls by. Make it easy for visitors to linger by creating a separate entry and exit for your booth if space permits.

If children will be present, keep them diverted with simple activities such as coloring contests, as doing that will create more time to talk to their parents.

Your goal is to stand out from the crowd. Keep these tips in mind:

★ A few minutes spent building rapport with a smaller number of people is a smarter strategy than taking home a bunch of anonymous leads. Collecting business cards by offering a chance to win a prize drawing may yield a lot of names, but you can expect meager results from your follow-up calls.

★ Giving consultations or samples without asking for contact details is throwing money away. Always get a name, cell phone number, and e-mail address so that you can follow up—no exceptions.

★ The more buzz you create, the more people will visit your booth. Make sure they linger long enough to build rapport by incorporating fun, interactive activities into your booth:

✓ Mini-facials!
✓ Accessorizing makeovers!
✓ Tasting tables!
✓ Guess the fragrances!
✓ Mini health checkups!
✓ Nutritional checkups!
✓ What's your fashion style?
✓ What's your cooking style?
✓ What's your home decor style?
✓ Are you guilty of the seven sins of skincare?
✓ Free samples!
✓ Cooking demonstrations!
✓ Gifts for the kids!
✓ Quick-fire quizzes!

★ If you're offering onsite consultations, create a "no-waiting" appointment list and invite event attendees to book a specific time to return for the consultation. Increase your chances of their returning by giving each person a ticket for a prize drawing.

★ Don't become so engaged with one person that you neglect others. Avoid the problem by having enough team members on-site to man the booth with you. If you're all busy and a new person drops by, make eye contact, smile, and say, *Thanks for waiting. I'll be with you in a minute.*

★ Stand out by outfitting your event team in company clothing and logos. The more your brand name is displayed the better.

★ Put your brightest lights at the front to draw in the crowd, but don't wait for people to come to you. If expo rules permit, send helpers into the crowd to offer free samples or discount coupons and invite people to drop by.

Less is more when it comes to your product display. You're at the event to attract customers, hosts, and business leads so don't put the spotlight solely on your products. Pop your business and party materials into brightly colored bags and top them with tissue for extra eye appeal. Stack them along the back of the booth to attract attention and act as conversation starters.

Increase the fun factor by adding an instant gift, cash voucher, makeover, treatment, or consultation coupon randomly to each bag and inviting qualified prospects to choose their own bags when they book a party or business appointment at the event.

Stay focused on your main purpose for being at the event, and that's to generate qualified leads for follow-up. Practice what you learned in Chapters 4 and 5.

★ Connect
★ Communicate
★ Continue

CREATE YOUR OWN SHOW

If you've built a network of direct selling professionals you can organize your own trade shows.

Form an organizing committee of your most enthused and

organized contacts to drive the project, and allocate tasks according to skills, experience, and connections with key suppliers.

The more vendors who participate, the more potential customers and recruits will walk through the door. Make attendance everyone's highest priority.

If an event is worth doing, it's worth doing well. Decorate the room and offer inexpensive enticements. Piping hot chocolate in winter, ice cold drinks in summer, lucky dips for the kids, and exclusive offers that can only be redeemed at the event will help draw the crowds.

Lower your costs by inviting sponsorships from local businesses. Banks, accounting firms, office suppliers, and retailers you support should jump at the chance to rub shoulders with successful entrepreneurs. The more value you offer the more people will attend, and if your giveaways are donated by willing sponsors your costs will be lower.

Invite the mayor to pop in (every person in public office needs to be seen). Turn it into a photo opportunity and try to garner some free publicity.

SOCIAL MEDIA

Social media is the fastest, cheapest way to spread the word, but it's a crowded arena.

If you are developing a serious e-strategy, you have access to unlimited resources to make your marketing messages pop. If social media plays a support role in your marketing efforts, start by adopting the recommendations outlined in Chapter 18.

Keep up with innovations by being alert to the e-communications you receive. When something impresses you, implement it in your e-marketing initiatives.

Remember, however, that social media can't do your job for you. The real action in direct selling takes place when you're standing two feet from your target.

FUND-RAISERS

Nonprofits are always short of funds, so you'll have many choices when it comes to deciding where to offer your support. Schools, preschools, sports teams, performance groups, scout troops, and community support programs are prime targets for fund-raisers, and if you do a good job they could become annual events.

Live fund-raising events will yield more networking opportunities but will take more time and effort. They're a great way to showcase your business, and the more value you offer the more people will show up. Although your products will ultimately determine whether you offer demonstrations, tastings, consultations, or fashion shows, it will pay to do everything you can to increase the appeal of attending.

Third-party fund-raisers at which you distribute product catalogs and order forms through the organization's support network in exchange for donating a portion of your proceeds to the organization will take less time. You will almost certainly boost your sales if you promote it well and make it easy to order, but you'll have to work harder to create contacts.

In both cases it's all about the numbers. Get the organizers on board by sharing the numbers up front when you present your proposition. For example, one hundred participants purchasing an average of $50 each will generate $5,000 in sales. If your donation is set at 20 percent, the organization will earn $1,000.

The more motivated the organization is the more it will get behind the fund-raiser. Choose a cause that has immediacy, for example, *Help our cheerleaders compete in the State Finals this fall.*

The key to a successful fund-raiser is simplicity, and the less stress you place on the organizer the more likely you will be invited back.

Donating a percentage of the proceeds of your own party sales to a worthy cause is another simple way to raise your profile. You'll increase your chances of media coverage if you make it a team effort and send out press releases with catchy headlines:

Local Businesses Unite to Support Military Families
Enterprising Entrepreneurs Organize Holiday Gift Fair
Empty Main Street Store Becomes Holiday Season Wonderland
Craft Workshops Make for Family Fun This Summer

SPEAK UP

Communicating is your business, and every entrepreneur has an interesting story to tell. Contact local professional and service groups and offer to speak at their meetings. If you're entertaining and interesting you'll be welcome everywhere.

Don't appear over-eager. Offer dates at least three to four months ahead. You don't want to be the last-minute booking or the back-up speaker if another speaker drops out. Be ready with your photo, bio, and an outline of your presentation before you make contact. Do your homework by finding out as much as possible about the group. No one wants to hear a cookie-cutter presentation.

Resist the urge to make a blatant pitch for your business. Your goal is to make new contacts and build relationships, so think long-term.

The more organized and professional you are to deal with, and the more interesting and entertaining you are at the event, the more likely you'll be invited to speak to other groups.

WRITE IT DOWN

Seeing your name and words in print will give your business and your morale a boost. While your story has to be relevant to the publication's audience, the reality is that most journalists appreciate having an interesting, topical story handed to them on a plate.

Readers appreciate fresh perspectives on current issues, but keep in mind that one-sided views will not impress anyone. If you're writing about the advantages of a home-based business, for example, make sure you share not only the benefits but also the challenges, such as staying focused and avoiding distractions. You can't be one-dimensional and interesting at the same time.

Don't shy away from sharing your success. Your story may inspire others to step up and change their lives:

I Partied Our Family Out of Debt
Fund-Raiser Nets Girl's Soccer Team $2,000
We Saved Our Home
Three Local Moms Win Free Cruise
Hometown Entrepreneur Earns National Title

Familiarize yourself with the readership, "voice," and typical article length of a publication before you send in your submission, and be sure to follow the three rules of good writing:

1. Edit!
2. Edit!
3. Edit!

Shoddy writing is an insult to readers. Because it's difficult to edit your own writing, it always pays to ask someone else to run an objective eye over your prized piece before you submit it.

An action photo will dramatically improve the odds of your article making it to print; a boring mug shot or product photograph will not. Make sure that your photo is a high-resolution image or you will have no chance of it being published.

MARKET YOURSELF

The most effective way to market your business is to market yourself every day as you go about your personal and business activity.

Being courteous, professional, and interested in others in your everyday dealings will make a positive impression on everyone you meet.

Don't keep your business a secret. Always let people know what you do and the company you're partnered with. Then, when those people think of your company, they'll think of you. When they think of your product, they'll think of you. When they think of someone they enjoy doing business with, they'll think of you.

The more visibility, respect, and likability you have in your community, the faster you'll grow. That is the magic of marketing.

CHAPTER TWENTY

Work with Integrity

Know what you stand for and stand for what you know.
—MARY CHRISTENSEN

The qualities you draw on to start your business are not the qualities that will sustain your success long term. Enthusiasm and energy are great business starters, but you won't be in business for the long haul without a strong set of values.

Your values define who you are and how you run your business. By operating your business with authenticity and integrity you'll attract the right people and be a leader they can respect, admire, and trust. Respect doesn't come with the title. Respect has to be earned. No matter how professional your image, or how sharp your communication skills, you will ultimately be measured by what you do. You won't be respected or trusted if your values can be shaped by prevailing winds.

Build, lead, and manage your business on an unshakable foundation of trust that comes from being credible, sincere, and consistent. When you know what you stand for it will be easier to run your business. Good actions follow good decisions, and good decisions come from having good values.

The following checklists will help you evaluate your credibility, sincerity, and consistency.

TEST YOUR CREDIBILITY:

☐ Am I proud of what I do?
☐ Do I express my pride openly and often?
☐ Am I friendly and approachable?
☐ Am I quick to praise and slow to complain?
☐ Do I follow through on my promises?
☐ Do I take responsibility for my actions?
☐ Do I apologize for my mistakes?
☐ Do I compliment often?

TEST YOUR SINCERITY:

☐ Can I be counted on to keep my word?
☐ Do I show a genuine interest in others?
☐ Am I concerned for the feelings of others?
☐ Do I value the opinions of others?
☐ Do I stand up for my beliefs?
☐ Do I refuse to gossip?
☐ Do I forgive easily?
☐ Do I give freely?
☐ Am I as kind to myself as I am to others?

TEST YOUR CONSISTENCY:

☐ Do I treat everyone with equal respect?
☐ Do I do the right thing always, not just when it's convenient?
☐ Am I the same person every time, and with everyone?
☐ Do I give the same service to everyone, every time?
☐ Do I always perform to the best of my ability?
☐ Am I grateful for what I have?
☐ Am I happy when others succeed?
☐ Do I walk the talk?

BUILD INTEGRITY INTO EVERY LAYER OF YOUR BUSINESS

Integrity is not something you can turn on and off at will. If you disparage the company, knock your competitors, oversell your opportunity, make exaggerated claims about your products, or disrespect service providers, you'll be perceived as a phony.

As Albert Einstein said: *"Whoever is careless with the truth in small matters cannot be trusted with important matters."*

There are many ways to incorporate integrity into your business:

★ Demonstrate that you stand for more than profit by giving generously. If you can't afford to give financially, donate your time.

★ Always give more than you take. We do business with people we respect, so plan to make at least one contribution to your community each year. One simple way to carry this out is to rally the team to support local businesses.

★ Make a list of restaurants, coffee shops, retailers, banks, gas stations, body shops, spas, nail clinics, and beauty salons and then set a team challenge to spend money at as many of those businesses as possible in one day.

★ Encourage your team to wear matching outfits, and deck your vehicles with business banners for maximum impact. Prepare simple cards that include your name, contact details, and a simple message, such as "We support local businesses," to hand out everywhere you go.

★ Get spouses, friends, and children involved to increase the number of businesses you reach, and expand the campaign by including a visit to the local fire station, sheriff's office, or police department to deliver appreciation cookies.

★ A similar campaign is to choose a day to perform an act of kindness in your community. Clean up the local park or deliver gifts to the residents of an assisted living facility. You can't go wrong by operating your business in a spirit of gratitude, generosity, and goodwill.

★ If your product lends itself to the practice, attach small samples to your business card to ensure that your company is remembered.

★ Be generous to your direct selling colleagues by not running your meetings as a secret society. Invite those who don't have a sponsor in the area to attend.

★ Be gracious when people decide to leave the business by thanking them for their contributions and wishing them well. Long after they have moved on they will remember how gracious you were.

★ Don't separate your personal and business standards. Follow this advice from respected advice columnist Ann Landers: *"The true measure of an individual is how he treats a person who can do him absolutely no good."*

★ Pay your bills on time, show courtesy behind the wheel, and tip generously.

MAINTAIN INTEGRITY WHEN THINGS GO WRONG

It's easy to be nice when things are going well, but the true measure of your leadership skills will be how well you keep your cool in difficult situations. Direct selling is a people business, and that makes it volatile. Even if you didn't create the problem, take ownership of it and control the solution.

If conflict arises, don't take it personally and don't make it personal. Anyone can stay upbeat when things are flowing smoothly. It's how you tackle the tough challenges that will show the world your true colors.

Let's examine an uncommon but scary scenario that could happen to any business owner:

Problem: One of your leaders leaves to join another company and starts approaching others in your organization to follow her.

Solution: Your first, instinctive response will most likely be fear about what this will mean for your business. This is natural. You have been betrayed from within your own ranks. What matters now is not to let the wound that has been inflicted become a fatal blow.

The direct selling industry is littered with the distant memory of people who lacked the loyalty gene needed to sustain success long term. In a last-ditch attempt to succeed, one of the short-term solutions these people may explore is switching allegiance to another company. This can happen in any business, and direct selling is no exception.

Their problem is greater than yours, because they will take with them the same absence of integrity and ethics that caused them to abuse your trust in the first place. In the long term, you're better off without them.

In the short term, however, you have to step up and take control. By acting in accordance with your own high ethical standards you will come out on top. Here is what I suggest:

★ Do not give up. In the short term you may lose some people, but you can, and will, rebuild if you follow the principles outlined in this book.

★ Don't waste time dwelling on your disappointment. This is a time to show leadership, and the image you project is critical. Put your hurt behind you and focus on being proactive and positive.

★ Don't make it personal. You are above shouting matches and retaliation.

★ When you confront the team member who is causing the problem do it in private, and start the conversation by expressing your willingness to work it out amicably.

★ Seek support from your upline, or find someone in your company to help you work through the issue. Even having someone to talk to will help.

★ Step up to the plate. Call everyone on your team and talk it through. Answer their questions openly and honestly. Stay calm and confident as you reaffirm your commitment to their success, and reassure them that it's business as usual.

★ Use the experience to strengthen your relationship with your team. By strengthening your relationships, you'll fortify your business against a future attack.

★ Above all, don't neglect your core business. A full calendar of personal activity will ensure that your business continues to thrive.

This is an extreme scenario, and not every situation is as dire. When small things go awry, try to look on the bright side. Humor was invented to keep challenges in perspective.

If you doubt any action you're considering, run it past these simple tests. The answers will tell you exactly what to do:

★ The billboard test—if your actions were advertised on a billboard in Times Square, would you be happy that others could see them?

★ The mirror test—when you look in the mirror, are you proud of the person staring back at you?

★ The switch test—if the tables were turned, would you be happy with how the situation played out?

It's not enough to be doing it. You have to be seen to be doing it. You can't have two sets of business values and earn respect. No one expects you to always be right, but they do expect you to be genuine.

You have the greatest stake in your business, so take personal responsibility for everything that happens, good and bad. Never blame others, even if they fall flat on their promises. You can't look for blame and solutions at the same time.

Some failure is inevitable, and every failure is an opportunity to learn. If you haven't failed, you haven't stretched yourself.

You have the power to choose how you work and with whom you work, but your team members bring a wide range of values to your organization. Although you cannot control everything they do, you can establish a clear list of acceptable and unacceptable behaviors for your group by making respect for others the backbone of your business.

By taking a black-and-white approach to personal and business ethics you'll earn the respect you deserve, and your impeccable standards will filter right through your organization.

CHAPTER TWENTY-ONE

Be Moneywise

Treat your business like a business.
—Mary Christensen

Home-based businesses come with significant financial advantages. Not only can you control how much you earn; you can control how much you keep. By managing your money wisely you'll earn more, save more, and keep more of your hard-earned cash.

KEEP PERSONAL AND BUSINESS FINANCES SEPARATE

Operate separate credit card, debit card, and checking accounts for your business and pay yourself a weekly allowance. If you need more, transfer the funds from your business to your personal account first.

Don't make the rookie mistake of treating your income as your personal piggy bank. If you dip into it to pay for groceries, snacks, or treats for the kids, it can evaporate quickly and you'll never know how much you're earning.

When I'm asked for help on dealing with unsupportive spouses, I often discover their concern is that the business is not making money. When the bank statements show money going out and not much coming in, spouses are understandably concerned. Showing them the money may be all it takes to get their support, so don't fritter away your income before it reaches your bank account.

LEGITIMIZE YOUR BUSINESS

Make sure you have the appropriate registrations, business licenses, and insurances. Your local city hall is the most reliable place for advice on what registrations and licenses you need.

DON'T WASTE MONEY

Any self-made millionaire will tell you to keep a close eye on expenses. Don't let your earnings be swallowed up by unnecessary extravagance or by negligence:

- ★ Regularly review what you're paying for basic services such as phone and Internet. It's a highly competitive market so there is always an abundance of deals that you can capitalize on to pay less and get more. If you make changes, be sure you notify everyone!
- ★ Reduce your home, business, and auto insurance premiums by opting for a higher deductible and taking advantage of the "bundle" discounts most insurers offer if you place all your policies with them.
- ★ Don't get carried away when the corporation advertises product specials. Buy only what you can consume or sell within three months. If you like to keep a few items on hand, focus on the fast movers.
- ★ Seek out cheaper suppliers for business essentials, but buy *when* things are on special, not *because* they are on special.

★ Don't buy more business supplies than you need. Bulk is fine for fast turnover items, but a buying-in-bulk strategy is flawed if it takes too long to use the supplies.

★ Don't waste ink and paper. Think twice before you print anything, select the "fast draft" option for most documents, and print on both sides of the paper. Recycle documents you have finished with as scrap paper.

★ Negotiate with hotels when you book their meeting rooms. If you can't reduce the price, you may be able to negotiate free nights, which you can use as rewards or incentives. A cheaper option is to approach local businesses and clubs about using their facilities.

★ Don't be above clipping coupons. If you print two coupons and pass one to a shopper browsing in the same aisle or standing next in line at the checkout, you may create a new contact. Thoughtful gestures make great conversation starters, and squandering opportunities is the same as squandering money.

★ Don't squander your time either. You need those hours to build your business. Prepare business materials in bulk, combine several errands in one trip, keep phone conversations short, and remember to spend the majority of your time with those who deserve it, not those who demand it.

★ Look for ways to curb your mileage. Every unnecessary trip raises the cost of running your business.

DECREASE YOUR TAX BILL

The greatest opportunity to maximize your income comes from paying less tax. Not taking advantage of all your expense deductions makes as little sense as returning your bonus check.

Keep proper records of your expenses. The rule-of-thumb is that if the expense was incurred in earning your income, you can claim it.

Pay by debit card, credit card, or electronic transfer where possible to create a clear trail of expenses, and always assume you will be asked to prove that the purchase was a legitimate business expense. Immediately record the reason for the expenditure and file all your receipts and statements at least once a month.

Request receipts when you pay cash for small items, as even the smallest expenses will add up over a year. At the end of every month, place the cash receipts in an envelope and reimburse yourself for the amount. Otherwise you'll be scrambling through scraps of paper at the end of the year to prepare your tax return.

Your largest deductions will most likely be your home office costs. To claim a home office deduction, your office space must be used exclusively and regularly for business. Big-ticket items such as computers, phones, and printers are also deductible if you purchased them for your business.

Ongoing expenses such as insurances and utilities, trash collection, and security can be claimed according to the percentage of your home that is dedicated office space.

The same calculation applies to expenses such as cleaning and general maintenance. You may even be able to claim the cost of furniture and refurbishing your office space.

Business use of your car will be a major business expense. Keep an accurate log of every business trip you make, and claim your mileage at the rate allowed by the government. The rate changes often, so check the current rate by searching *mileage rate*.

If you use your car more than 50 percent of the time for business you may be able to claim a percentage of all your car expenses. Keep a log of all your business trips, and copies of all your gasoline, licensing, insurance, repair, and maintenance expenses, so the business deduction can be accurately calculated as a percentage of your total car expenses.

You can claim the cost of attending your company's national convention, leadership conferences, and other training events. Allowable expenses include airline tickets, taxis, shuttle transfers, hotels, rental cars, accommodations, and meals. Keep a day-to-day log of your activities while you're away to prove the legitimacy of your trip. Some tax advisers recommend you keep the convention program as proof that you participated in a legitimate business event.

Although your CPA will be your best resource for tax advice, you can be reasonably sure that the myriad of claimable expenses include business licenses; telephone service; marketing, promotional, and training materials; stationery, printing, and copying; outside contractors; advertising; registration fees for training courses and seminars; Internet connection; website creation, hosting, and maintenance; bank fees and interest paid on business loans and expenses; products you use for demonstration or sampling; gifts, incentives, and prizes; professional fees such as accounting, bookkeeping, preparing tax returns, and legal fees; health, medical, life, and personal liability insurances; professional and networking association memberships; subscriptions to relevant magazines and newspapers; and charitable donations.

Take advantage of all possible savings available to self-employed people by funneling as much as you can afford into a self-employed retirement fund.

Be sure to submit your tax return on time and pay your taxes before the due date. If you hire a professional tax adviser, choose one who has experience with self-employed clients. Do not, however, abdicate your responsibilities to a third party. Tax advisers work with the information you give them, and it is your responsibility to know what you can and cannot claim.

The more you know, the more confident you'll be when submitting your tax returns. The most reliable site for information on your responsibilities as a small-business owner is www.irs.gov/businesses/small/index.html.

You work hard to earn your income, and you deserve to keep it. By taking your rights and obligations seriously you'll enjoy the satisfaction of knowing you paid what you owed and not a cent more.

MAKE YOUR MONEY MATTER

How different would your life be if you were free of debt?

Debt destroys the reason most of us start a business, which is to achieve financial freedom. You sacrifice that freedom by overloading yourself with debt.

Build a debt reduction plan into your business. Pay the full balance on your credit cards and think twice before you borrow to buy anything you can't afford to pay for in full. Safeguard your family by putting a percentage of your earnings in an emergency fund to cover unexpected expenses or challenges. Think about how you'll survive if you're unable to work, your spouse loses his or her job, or one of you needs long-term healthcare or dies. Not having an emergency fund to pay the bills if the money stops flowing in is foolish.

Treat your business as a business, and apply as much discipline to managing your money as you do to making it. Don't squander it on wasteful, unnecessary, or precipitous spending. Push the pause button and think, *Do I really need this?* before you reach for your wallet. By practicing restraint now you'll accumulate enough money for bigger and better rewards down the line.

Conclusion

Congratulations! This book has equipped you with the knowledge you need to reach the highest rank and rewards in your company's compensation plan. It's time to apply what you've learned so you can reap the rewards that flow to those who reach the highest levels of the plan.

Knowledge is never enough. Even the brightest student will tell you that graduation day signals the start of the journey, not the end. It's what you do with what you know that makes the difference.

Only the most dedicated direct sellers will travel all the way to the top of the plan! You will need every ounce of determination, discipline, and drive to be one of them.

These are the same qualities that produce winners in every field of endeavor, from academia and business to sports and entertainment. What separates the dreamers from the doers is an unshakable commitment to completing the journey.

My hero as a child growing up in New Zealand was Sir Edmund Hillary, the first man ever to climb Mt. Everest, the world's highest mountain. His achievement made him a national idol, and inspired many New Zealanders to realize that it doesn't matter where you come from; it's where you want to go that matters. If we want it and are willing to work for it, perhaps we too could achieve greatness.

Mt. Everest rises a majestic 29,000 feet above sea level, and it's a magnet for every adventurer who dreams of standing on top of the world.

Reaching the summit is not a challenge for the fainthearted, but that doesn't dissuade hundreds of climbers from attempting the ascent each year. Completing the first stage of the climb to Base Camp is an accomplishment in itself, and an important milestone on every climber's journey to the top of the world.

Despite its name, North Face Base Camp is not at the base of the mountain but 17,000 feet above sea level. Every climber who reaches it has already displayed the mental and physical stamina needed to reach the summit. However, no amount of planning or preparation can predict how the next stage of the journey will play out. Mt. Everest has its own ecosystem, and no one knows what conditions they will experience on any given day, minute, or second. The only certainty climbers can count on is complete, total uncertainty.

Conditions may be perfect when they set out from Base Camp. Then halfway to the summit the weather closes in and they have no choice other than to retreat.

When the storm passes they will make another attempt to complete that last 12,000 feet. But there's every chance the storm will have left behind fresh challenges. Walls of ice may block the route they planned to take, and they will have to find an alternative way up the mountain. Avalanches, hidden crevasses, dense clouds, and driving sleet will test the stamina of even the fittest climber.

Every climber knows that you cannot control conditions on the mountain, but you can control how you confront the challenges it delivers. What keeps the climber pressing forward is a goal worth fighting for, and a determination to reach it, no matter how many challenges there are along the way.

It's the same in business. The difference between success and failure is persistence. However how long it takes, and whatever happens, never give in.

Equip yourself with a goal worth working for, and a determination to achieve it. Accept that having a planned strategy doesn't mean you can afford to be inflexible. Unforeseen changes are not only inevitable, they are a golden opportunity to strengthen your skills so that you are better equipped for the next challenge.

The global economy is experiencing tough times right now, but the direct selling industry is outpacing growth in just about every country worldwide. That people are seeking the opportunity you offer is evident in the numbers.

In 2012, the World Federation of Direct Selling Associations (WFDSA) released annual statistics indicating that the direct selling industry grew 10 percent worldwide to just under $154 billion gross sales.

In the United States direct selling grew 4.6 percent, significantly outpacing the overall economy, which grew 3.9 percent in the same period. In Australia, direct selling has averaged annual sales growth of 12.5 percent for the past three years, compared with growth of 4.1 percent for the overall retail sector in the same period.

The longer you are in business, the more you can expect to experience economic upswings and downswings. Your personal circumstances are also likely to fluctuate, as will the growth of your business. Sometimes you will feel that you are moving in the fast lane and at other times you will think that you are stalled, or stuck in the slow lane.

You have to be willing to respond to the circumstances you encounter and not allow yourself to be defeated when things don't go according to plan. You cannot expect to keep doing things the same way and achieve a different result. When conditions change, you must change.

The only thing you can't afford to change is your commitment to your goal. You have a responsibility to the people you introduced to the business to be the best you can be and to not let disappointment, distractions, and unplanned detours defeat you on your ascent to the top.

Give yourself permission to succeed, and be true to your word by shedding the attitudes and actions that will halt your progress.

Don't be afraid to fail. You won't conquer challenges unless you're willing to take risks. As Erica Jong so aptly said: *"The trouble is, if you don't risk anything, you risk even more."*

Leaders never stop growing. They are constantly looking for ways to improve themselves. When you feel fear or frustration, don't expect the people around you to change, and don't expect the circumstances to change. You must change.

No matter how much you want it, and how much you work at it, you will not grow if you keep repeating your mistakes. Don't be so busy working in your business that there's no time to step back and evaluate what you are doing. New ideas will refresh and revitalize your business. When something is not working for you, do something else.

Start every year by asking:

What will I do the same as last year?
What will I do better than last year?
What will I do differently?

It's natural to feel uncertain or apprehensive at times, so don't be afraid to show your vulnerable side. To disguise parts of our personality is a form of dishonesty. Be proud of who you are and how you arrived here, but be willing to keep growing.

One of the biggest challenges the direct selling profession faces comes from leaders who have been successful but are unable or unwilling to upgrade their skills to support future generations. When you stop growing you become a liability to the business, just as any CEO who ceases to lead becomes a liability.

Never stop looking for ways you can grow personally, and never stop looking for ways to run your business more effectively. Your business gives you the power to change lives. Start by doing everything you can to be the best you can be.

> *It's not the mountain we must*
> *conquer—but ourselves.*
> —SIR EDMUND HILLARY

INDEX

ABOUT THE AUTHOR

Mary Christensen is direct selling's number-one speaker and author worldwide. Her bestselling books *Be a Party Plan Superstar*, *Be a Network Marketing Superstar*, and *Be a Recruiting Superstar* are available in many languages, including Spanish, French, Indonesian, and Bulgarian.

Mary Christensen travels the world making presentations to direct selling audiences, and her live leadership programs have equipped thousands of direct selling leaders to succeed. She works with many of the industry's most successful direct selling corporations to empower and equip their leaders for success.

Mary Christensen left teaching to start her first direct selling business and soon after founded her own company. She has walked the talk and has the credibility of success in every aspect of direct sales leadership. She is a former CEO of two direct selling corporations and past President of the Direct Selling Association (NZ).

Direct Selling Live named Mary Christensen one of the ten most influential women in direct selling worldwide, and The Multilevel Marketing International Association (MLMIA) honored her as their Best of the Best Worldwide Award recipient.

When she is not speaking, Mary Christensen lives in Monterey, California. You can email her at mary_christensen@live.com or join her on Facebook at http://www.facebook.com/pages/Mary-Christensen/211 167465605116?sk=wall.

Also by Direct Selling Expert Mary Christensen

Be a Network Marketing Superstar:
The One Book You Need to Make More Money
Than You Ever Thought Possible

A step-by-step guide to mastering the proven wealth-building techniques that top earners use to become network marketing stars!

Price: $15.00
ISBN: 9780814474310
Format: Paperback

Be a Party Plan Superstar:
Build a $100,000-a-Year Direct Selling Business from Home

Let's get this party started! This one-of-a-kind guide shows direct sellers how to build and expand their party plan business.

Price: $17.95
ISBN: 9780814416518
Format: Paperback

Be a Recruiting Superstar:
The Fast Track to Network Marketing Millions

The proven recruiting techniques to take network marketing pros to a whole new level!

Price: $16.00
ISBN: 9780814401637
Format: Paperback

Mary's books have been translated into five languages.

Visit Mary's website:
http://www.marychristensen.com/

Print edition details as noted. Most AMACOM titles are also available as eBooks. Please visit your favorite eBook supplier for pricing.

For more about these titles and other AMACOM titles visit our website:
www.amacombooks.org